Nancy G. Klimas, MD
Roberto Patarca, MD, PhD
Editors

Disability and Chronic Fatigue Syndrome

Clinical, Legal and Patient Perspectives

Disability and Chronic Fatigue Syndrome: Clinical, Legal and Patient Perspectives has been co-published simultaneously as *Journal of Chronic Fatigue Syndrome*, Volume 3, Number 4 1997.

Pre-publication
REVIEWS,
COMMENTARIES,
EVALUATIONS . . .

"**D**isability and Chronic Fatigue Syndrome: Clinical, Legal and Patient Perspectives fills an important niche for physicians and health care providers dealing with the problem of overriding fatigue. A group of well-respected experts in the field of fatigue present lucid descriptions and recommendations on how fatigue and disability can be measured. Most importantly, the book's contributors reflect an appreciation of the overlap between psychological (and cognitive) and physical symptoms associated with fatigue. The reader gains an understanding of the impact fatigue has on populations and the extent to which this disease entity can limit productivity and affect normal activity. *Disability and Chronic Fatigue Syndrome: Clinical, Legal and Patient Perspectives* provides helpful information for clinicians dealing with long-term disability problems stemming from chronic fatigue syndrome and other chronic diseases. The overall description of the chronic fatigue syndrome, its impact on the health of populations, and its challenge to physicians, are handled in this volume in a very helpful and valuable manner."

Jay A. Levy, MD
Professor of Medicine
University of California,
San Francisco

"**A**s a physician who deals with disability issues daily, I found this volume fascinating and informative. Once I started reading I couldn't put the book down!

This volume is a complete overview of disability, including a primer on social security, advice from a practicing attorney, and approach to disability for clinicians, research articles, and even personal experience. The scientific papers give credibility to the disability process, . . .

This is "must read" material for anyone involved with the disability process and CFS."

Charles W. Lapp, MD
Director
Hunter-Hopkins Center
Charlotte, North Carolina

"**L**ike a good mystery novel, *Disability and Chronic Fatigue Syndrome: Clinical, Legal and Patient Perspectives* is full of clues to help solve the scientific riddle of those disabled by CFS.

From the perspective of the players–the patient, the physician, the psychologist, the attorney, the rehabilitation specialist, and the government agency–the reader develops a full appreciation of the necessity for a multi-disciplinary approach to the problem.

Whether you believe that CFS is a viable entity or not, *Disability and Chronic Fatigue Syndrome: Clinical, Legal and Patient Perspectives* offers an excellent analysis of this complex impairment. It belongs on every disability bookshelf."

Lyle D. Lieberman
Attorney
Former U.S. Administrative Law Judge
Social Security Administration

The Haworth Medical Press
An Imprint of The Haworth Press, Inc.

Disability and Chronic Fatigue Syndrome

Clinical, Legal and Patient Perspectives

Disability and Chronic Fatigue Syndrome: Clinical, Legal and Patient Perspectives has been co-published simultaneously as *Journal of Chronic Fatigue Syndrome*, Volume 3, Number 4 1997.

Disability and Chronic Fatigue Syndrome

Clinical, Legal and Patient Perspectives

Nancy G. Klimas, MD
Roberto Patarca, MD, PhD
Editors

Disability and Chronic Fatigue Syndrome: Clinical, Legal and Patient Perspectives has been co-published simultaneously as *Journal of Chronic Fatigue Syndrome*, Volume 3, Number 4 1997.

The Haworth Medical Press
An Imprint of
The Haworth Press, Inc.
New York • London

Published by

The Haworth Medical Press, 10 Alice Street, Binghamton, NY 13904-1580 USA

The Haworth Medical Press is an imprint of The Haworth Press, Inc., 10 Alice Street, Binghamton, NY 13904-1580 USA.

Disability and Chronic Fatigue Syndrome: Clinical, Legal and Patient Perspectives has been co-published simultaneously as *Journal of Chronic Fatigue Syndrome*, Volume 3, Number 4 1997.

Cover design by Thomas J. Mayshock Jr.

Library of Congress Cataloging-in-Publication Data

Disability and chronic fatigue syndrome: clinical, legal, and patient perspectives / Nancy G. Klimas, Roberto Patarca, editors.
     p. cm.–(Journal of chronic fatigue syndrome; v. 3, no. 4)
     Includes bibliographical references and index.
     ISBN 0-7890-0393-7 (alk. paper).–ISBN 0-7890-0501-8 (pbk.: alk. paper)
     1. Chronic fatigue syndrome. 2. Disability evaluation. 3. Chronic fatigue syndrome–Law and legislation–United States. I. Klimas, Nancy G., 1954- . II. Patarca, Roberto. III. Series.
     [DNLM: 1. Fatigue Syndrome, Chronic–complications. 2. Disability Evaluation. W1 JO585W v. 3 no. 4 1997 / WB 146D611 1997]
RB150.F37D57 1997
616'.0478–DC21
DNLM/DLC
for Library of Congress
                                  97-42720
                                       CIP

INDEXING & ABSTRACTING

Contributions to this publication are selectively indexed or abstracted in print, electronic, online, or CD-ROM version(s) of the reference tools and information services listed below. This list is current as of the copyright date of this publication. See the end of this section for additional notes.

- *Abstracts in Anthropology,* Baywood Publishing Company, 26 Austin Avenue, P.O. Box 337, Amityville, NY 11701

- *Abstracts of Research in Pastoral Care & Counseling,* Loyola College, 7135 Minstrel Way, Suite 101, Columbia, MD 21045

- *Academic Abstracts/CD-ROM,* EBSCO Publishing Editorial Department, P.O. Box 590, Ipswich, MA 01938-0590

- *AIDS Abstracts,* Carfax Publishing Company, P.O. Box 25, Abingdon, Oxfordshire OX14 3UE, United Kingdom

- *Behavioral Medicine Abstracts,* University of Washington, Department of Social Work & Speech & Hearing Sciences, Box 354900, Seattle, WA 98195

- *CFIDS Pathfinder,* P.O. Box 2644, Kensington, MD 20891-2644

- *CINAHL (Cumulative Index to Nursing & Allied Health Literature), in print, also on CD-ROM from CD PLUS, EBSCO, and SilverPlatter, and online from CDP Online (formerly BRS), Data-Star, and PaperChase. (Support materials include Subject Heading List, Database Search Guide, and instructional video),* CINAHL Information Systems, P.O. Box 871/1509 Wilson Terrace, Glendale, CA 91209-0871

- *CNPIEC Reference Guide: Chinese National Directory of Foreign Periodicals,* P.O. Box 88, Beijing, People's Republic of China

- *Dental Abstracts,* Mosby-Year Book, Inc., 161 N. Clark Street, Fl 1900, Chicago, IL 60601-3221

(continued)

- *Digest of Neurology and Psychiatry,* The Institute of Living, 400 Washington Street, Hartford, CT 06106

- *Excerpta Medica/Secondary Publishing Division,* Elsevier Science Inc., Secondary Publishing Division, 655 Avenue of the Americas, New York, NY 10010

- *Greenfiles,* 138 Oak Tree Lane, Nottinghamshire NG18 3HR, United Kingdom

- *Health Source: Indexing & Abstracting of 160 selected health related journals, updated monthly,* EBSCO Publishing, 83 Pine Street, Peabody, MA 01960

- *Health Source Plus: expanded version of "Health Source" to be released shortly,* EBSCO Publishing, 83 Pine Street, Peabody, MA 01960

- *Human Resources Abstracts (HRA),* Sage Publications, Inc., 2455 Teller Road, Newbury Park, CA 91320

- *Industrial Hygiene Digest,* Industrial Health Foundation, Inc., 34 Penn Circle West, Pittsburgh, PA 15206

- *INTERNET ACCESS (& additional networks) Bulletin Board for Libraries ("BUBL") coverage of information resources on INTERNET, JANET, and other networks.*
  - <URL:http://bubl.ac.uk/>
  - The new locations will be found under <URL:http://bubl.ac.uk/link/>.
  - Any existing BUBL users who have problems finding information on the new service should contact the BUBL help line by sending e-mail to <bubl@bubl.ac.uk>.
  The Andersonian Library, Curran Building, 101 St. James Road, Glasgow G4 0NS, Scotland

- *Journal of College Science Teaching (abstracts section),* California State University, Department of Chemistry, Fresno, CA 93740-0070

- *Leeds Medical Information,* University of Leeds, Leeds LS2 9JT, United Kingdom

(continued)

- **ME and CFS Medical Update (available from the British Library's Medical Information Centre),** 23 Melbourne Road, Teddington, Middlesex TW11 9QX, United Kingdom

- **Mental Health Abstracts (online through DIALOG),** IFI/Plenum Data Company, 3202 Kirkwood Highway, Wilmington, DE 19808

- **Nutrition Research Newsletter "Abstracts Section,"** Lyda Associates, Inc., P.O. Box 700, Palisades, NY 10964

- **PASCAL, %Institute de L'Information Scientifique et Technigue,** cross-disciplinary electronic database covering the fields of science, technology & medicine. Also available on CD-ROM, and can generate customized retrospective searches. For more information: INIST, Customer Desk, 2, allée du Parc de Brabois, F-54514 Vandoeuvre Cedex, France, http//www.inist.fr

- **Pharmacist's Letter "Abstracts Section,"** Therapeutic Research Center, P.O. Box 8190, Stockton, CA 95208-0190

- **Published International Literature on Traumatic Stress (The PILOTS Database),** National Center for Post-Traumatic Stress Disorder (116D), VA Medical Center, White River Junction, VT 05009

- **Referativnyi Zhurnal (Abstracts Journal of the Institute of Scientific Information of the Republic of Russia),** The Institute of Scientific Information, Baltijskaja ul., 14, Moscow A-219, Republic of Russia

- **REHABDATA, National Rehabilitation Information Center,** searches are available in large-print, cassette or Braille format and all are available on PC-compatible diskette (also accessible via the Internet at http//www.naric.com/naric.), 8455 Colesville Road, Suite 935, Silver Spring, MD 20910-3319

- **Sapient Health Network,** 720 SW Washington Street #400, Portland, OR 97205-3537

- **Selected Abstracts on Occupational Diseases (DHSSDATA),** The Industrial Injuries Advisory Council, A4 6th Floor, The Adelphi, 1-11 John Adams Street, London WC2N 6HT, England

(continued)

- *Sociological Abstracts (SA),* Sociological Abstracts, Inc., P.O. Box 22206, San Diego, CA 92192-0206

- *Violence and Abuse Abstracts: A Review of Current Literature on Interpersonal Violence (VAA),* Sage Publications, Inc., 2455 Teller Road, Newbury Park, CA 91320

SPECIAL BIBLIOGRAPHIC NOTES

related to special journal issues (separates)
and indexing/abstracting

☐ indexing/abstracting services in this list will also cover material in any "separate" that is co-published simultaneously with Haworth's special thematic journal issue or DocuSerial. Indexing/abstracting usually covers material at the article/chapter level.

☐ monographic co-editions are intended for either non-subscribers or libraries which intend to purchase a second copy for their circulating collections.

☐ monographic co-editions are reported to all jobbers/wholesalers/approval plans. The source journal is listed as the "series" to assist the prevention of duplicate purchasing in the same manner utilized for books-in-series.

☐ to facilitate user/access services all indexing/abstracting services are encouraged to utilize the co-indexing entry note indicated at the bottom of the first page of each article/chapter/contribution.

☐ this is intended to assist a library user of any reference tool (whether print, electronic, online, or CD-ROM) to locate the monographic version if the library has purchased this version but not a subscription to the source journal.

☐ individual articles/chapters in any Haworth publication are also available through the Haworth Document Delivery Service (HDDS).

Disability
and Chronic Fatigue Syndrome

Clinical, Legal and Patient Perspectives

CONTENTS

ABOUT THE EDITORS

Nancy G. Klimas, MD, is Professor of Medicine at the University of Miami School of Medicine, where she is Director of the University's Diagnostic Immunology and Allergy Clinic and Co-Director of the E.M. Papper Clinical Immunology Laboratory. She is also Director of AIDS Research Unit of the Miami VA Medical Center. Dr. Klimas is Vice President of the American Association for Chronic Fatigue Syndrome and serves on the Medical Advisory Boards of the Chronic Fatigue and Immunodeficiency Syndrome Foundation and the National Association for Environmental Medicine Research. She has co-authored numerous journal articles and book chapters and is a frequent speaker at CFS conferences on the basis of her experience as both researcher and clinician.

Roberto Patarca, MD, PhD, HCLD, CC, TC, is Assistant Professor of Medicine, Microbiology, and Immunology and also serves as Research Director of the E.M. Papper Laboratory of Clinical Immunology at the University of Miami. Previously, he was Assistant Professor of Pathology at the Dana-Farber Cancer Institute and Harvard Medical School in Boston. Dr. Patarca also serves as Editor of *Critical Reviews in Oncogenesis* and is the author or co-author of more than 70 articles in journals or books. He is currently conducting research on the mechanisms of lymphomagenesis and cellular immunotherapy in AIDS and a study on pediatric AIDS, as well as research on chronic fatigue syndrome. Dr. Patarca is a member of the Board of Directors of the Acquired Non-HIV Immune Diseases Foundation, the American Association for the Advancement of Science, and the Clinical Immunology Society.

Introduction

Nancy G. Klimas

With this publication, we hope to open the door to the debate on equitable assessment of disability in CFS and equitable access to entitlement programs. In every meeting of patients, investigators, clinicians, and most recently the administrative law judges, the issue of disability and CFS is hotly debated. This book is a response to requests from many investigators and clinicians for a written forum to discuss Disability and Chronic Fatigue Syndrome.

In 1994 the International CFS Study Group was charged with developing a new CFS case definition. In doing so they described the illness in this way: "The chronic fatigue syndrome is a clinically defined condition characterized by severe disabling fatigue and a combination of symptoms that prominently features self-reported impairments in concentration and short-term memory, sleep disturbances, and musculo-skeletal pain" (1). Severely disabling fatigue is difficult to quantify. The 1994 case definition dropped the requirement of an "average daily activity below 50%" as difficult to verify, and described the fatigue as severe mental and physical exhaustion which is not attributable to exertion or diagnosable disease. Fatigue is not the only symptom contributing to a level of impairment or disability. Symptoms of cognitive dysfunction, pain, sleep disturbance, secondary depression and anxiety may all contribute at varying levels. The severity of illness may vary widely among the patient population: from the house-bound or bed-bound patient, to a less severely impacted patient able to work full or part time. Yet the usual clinical evaluation does not go far enough to develop an impairment rating. Existing scales, validated in the literature, include general health scales (e.g., Short Form-36 or the Sickness Impact Profile); cognitive assessment through a standard neurocogni-

[Haworth co-indexing entry note]: "Introduction." Klimas, Nancy G. Co-published simultaneously in *Journal of Chronic Fatigue Syndrome* (The Haworth Medical Press, an imprint of The Haworth Press, Inc.) Vol. 3, No. 4, 1997, pp. 1-3; and: *Disability and Chronic Fatigue Syndrome: Clinical, Legal and Patient Perspectives* (ed: Nancy G. Klimas, and Roberto Patarca) The Haworth Medical Press, an imprint of The Haworth Press, Inc., 1997, pp. 1-3. Single or multiple copies of this article are available for a fee from The Haworth Document Delivery Service [1-800-342-9678, 9:00 a.m. - 5:00 p.m. (EST). E-mail address: getinfo@haworth.com].

tive battery (see Dimitrov and Grafman article); pain quantification (visual analogue scales as well as careful tender point evaluations with dolometers); sleep studies and sleep disturbance scales; and psychometric testing of depression and anxiety. Recent articles by Buchwald et al. (2) and Komaroff et al. (3) describe the use of a variety of measures in determining severity of illness and degree of impairment. Studies by Natelson's group demonstrated post-exertional dramatic drops in cognitive capacity in a controlled study (4), another objective measure that could be used to demonstrate degree of impairment in an individual. Another intriguing possibility is the use of 2-5A-dependent RNase L activity as a laboratory measure as suggested by Suhadolnik and colleagues in a recent publication (5).

Studies such as that described by Peter Manu that depend on retrospective chart review for data are not designed to clarify the best method for assigning disability ratings, but highlight the paucity of objective data currently used in clinical practices in evaluating this illness. Donald Uslan's article reminds us that there are experts in rehabilitation that are expert in determining degree of impairment. His practical proposed guidelines encompass the many facets of this illness and give very reasonable guidelines in the assessment of disability in this population.

One would hope, taking this issue in its entirety, that the reader would conclude that more work should be done to develop objective measures of impairment that would accurately reflect the patient's degree of disability. Such an accomplishment would benefit the patient by hastening the disability claims process; lawyers and adjudicators in coming to equitable decisions; and clinicians by enabling them to more fully understand their patients and the severity of their illness.

In this forum authors bring a wide range of expertise to a tough problem. How can a clinician quantify the degree of impairment? How can the legal and judicial system weigh the facts and the impact of this illness on each person with CFS? And how does a patient persevere and get past the barriers, despite her/his illness? In many ways more questions have been raised than answered, but it's a start.

REFERENCES

1. Fukada K, Straus S, Hickie I, Sharpe M, Dobbins J, Komaroff, A and the Intl CFS Study Group. The chronic fatigue syndrome: A comprehensive approach to its definition and study. *Ann Intern Med* 1994; 121:953-959.

2. Buchwald D, Pearlamn T, Umali J, Schmaling K, Katon W. Functional status in patients with chronic fatigue syndrome, other fatiguing illnesses, and healthy individuals. *Am J Med* 1996; 171:364-370.

3. Komaroff AL, Fagioli LR, Doolittle TH, Gandek B, Gleit MA, Guerriero RT, Kornish RJ, Ware NC, Bates DW. Health status in patients with chronic fatigue syndrome and in general population and disease comparison groups. *Am J Med* 1996; 101:281-290.

4. LaManca J, DeLuca J, Johnson S, Lange G, Pareja J, Cook S, Sisto SA, Natelson B. Cognitive function in chronic fatigue syndrome (CFS) following exhaustive treadmill exercise. Presentation at the AACFS Conference, San Francisco, October, 1996.

5. Suhadolnik RJ, Peterson DL, O'Brien K, Cheney PR, Herst CVT, Reichenbach NL, Kon N, Horvath SE, Iacono KT, Adelson ME, De Meirleir K, DeBecker P, Charubala R, Pfleiderer W. Evidence for a novel low molecular weight 2-5A-dependent RNase L in chronic fatigue syndrome. *J Interferon & Cytokine Res* 1997; 17:377-385.

EDITORIALS

Chronic Fatigue Syndrome and Disability

Regardless of etiology and pathogenesis, the symptom complex labeled chronic fatigue syndrome (CFS) can and does result in prolonged moderate to severe disability. As the Centers for Disease Control (CDC) has acknowledged, the vast majority of patients recover in the first two years following onset of the illness and are unlikely to recover after five years. In the 10-year follow-up study conducted, approximately 20% of the initially evaluated patients with CFS remained moderately symptomatic at ten years (1). The illness at that point is, of course, confounded by the effects of chronic illness such as deconditioning, loss of employment, loss of relationships, and loss of income. The process thus becomes functionally disabling due to the multiplicity of symptoms and the profound perceived or actual inability to produce energy.

[Haworth co-indexing entry note]: "Chronic Fatigue Syndrome and Disability." Peterson, Daniel L. Co-published simultaneously in *Journal of Chronic Fatigue Syndrome* (The Haworth Medical Press, an imprint of The Haworth Press, Inc.) Vol. 3, No. 4, 1997, pp. 5-7; and: *Disability and Chronic Fatigue Syndrome: Clinical, Legal and Patient Perspectives* (ed: Nancy G. Klimas, and Roberto Patarca) The Haworth Medical Press, an imprint of The Haworth Press, Inc., 1997, pp. 5-7. Single or multiple copies of this article are available for a fee from The Haworth Document Delivery Service [1-800-342-9678, 9:00 a.m. - 5:00 p.m. (EST). E-mail address: getinfo@haworth.com].

The decision to seek legal disability benefits often results from an acute crisis or exacerbation of symptoms with subsequent failure of prior compensatory or coping strategies. Often effective strategies to avoid this "last resort" safety net approach may succeed and should be instituted early on and continued through the course of the illness. Examples of effective strategies include cognitive behavioral therapy, energy conservation programs, life style modifications, and extremely slowly progressive anaerobic exercise programs. When these methods, together with appropriate medical therapy fail, legal disability becomes the only viable mechanism of survival for many patients.

Those who hold a disability rights perspective view disabled people as a minority group subject to discrimination and unfair treatment. The charitable perspective views Patients With Chronic Fatigue Syndrome (PWCFS) as unfortunate and deserving of pity and care. They view PWCFS as needing to be "cured." Through passage of legislation such as the Americans with Disabilities Act (ADA), public policy has empowered the disability rights perspective. There has subsequently developed a disability culture geared to ensuring a common worldview (2).

Despite the power of the ADA and other technical assistance provided by the federal government, many physicians and patients are unaware of the requirements and benefits of the law. For many PWCFS to continue working becomes irrational. While there are well-established and funded systems to support PWCFS in dependency, there is little support for efforts to maintain independence. Few patients on Social Security return to work, although there exist mechanisms for trial employment, and thus a long lifetime of poverty is ensured.

Incentives built into managed care undermine physician and patient efforts at rehabilitation and independent living. Due to high costs, disturbing proposals and dialogue have emerged from the private and public disability sectors. Several very large private disability carriers recently announced plans to impose two year limits on benefits for diseases that are poorly characterized such as CFS. The ethical question for public policy then becomes "Can we afford disabled CFS people?" Diagnosis and treatment of disabled people has historically been the responsibility of the treating physicians. The third party payers are now performing these functions. The decisions are most often based on economic rather than medical or ethical criteria.

Solutions to this dilemma must include clarification of public policy. For example, national guidelines for diagnosis of CFS and related disorders, as well as guidelines for determination of disability, must be established. "Medical Necessity" must be redefined.

One objective and reproducible technique for determining and measuring functional disability that should be used consistently is Cardio-Pulmonary Exercise Testing with measurement of VO2 max, anaerobic threshold and maximal heart rate and respiration. The test is well established, sedentary and ill norms are published and the technology is relatively inexpensive and quite available. Approximately 1700 patients have been tested over the past ten years and the test is now used on the initial visit to screen patients, to direct rehabilitation, and adjunctively to determine disability (3,4).

Most importantly, long-term cost effectiveness should be evaluated from an individual and societal perspective, not just from a cost saving health plan perspective. Interventions should be developed to slow or reverse functional loss. Persons knowledgeable in CFS should determine medical necessity and medical disability. It is rare to read an Independent Medical Examination report that reflects any knowledge of the criteria for diagnosis or associated laboratory results seen in CFS. The very concept of independent medical examinations must be questioned when the examinations are extremely superficial and are bought and paid for by the third party payers. Objectivity is doubtful when fees for such exams may run as high as six to eight thousand dollars.

Public policy issues that surround chronic illness such as CFS are thorny, at best. Treating physicians must become knowledgeable about effective compensatory strategies that patients can use. Consistent and reliable methods for determining effectively disability must be initiated. Finally, disability rights advocates must actively oppose medical decisions based solely on immediate cost savings to third party payers.

Daniel L. Peterson, MD
Medical Director
UCSF Clinic
San Francisco, CA

REFERENCES

1. Hughes MD. Chronic fatigue syndrome: Prospects for pharmaceutical and diagnostic manufacturers. Spectrum: Decision Resources, Inc. February 21, 1996; 79:1-12.

2. National Council on Disability. Achieving independence: The challenge for the 21st century. July 26, 1996. Conference Chairperson: Marca Bristo.

3. Neuberg GW, Friedman SH, Weiss MB, Herman MV. Cardiopulmonary exercise testing: the clinical value of gas exchange data. *Arch Intern Med* 1988; 148: 2221-2226.

4. Sisto SA et al. Metabolic and cardiovascular effects of a progressive exercise test in patients with chronic fatigue syndrome. *Am J Med* 1996; 100:635-640.

Disability Evaluation
for Chronic Fatigue Syndrome

Occupational disability is common among patients given the diagnosis of chronic fatigue syndrome (CFS). In a recent study performed at the Chronic Fatigue Clinic of the University of Washington (1) the issue was addressed by measuring the employment status at the time of the initial examination and at follow-up 1.7 years (average) later. On both occasions, patients were asked if, during the last 3 months, they were able to remain at work on a full time or part time basis. The initial cohort consisted of 236 patients with a chief complaint of chronic fatigue who fulfilled criteria for CFS (147 patients, 81% women), fibromyalgia (28 patients, 89% women) or both (61 patients, 90% women). The duration of illness averaged 5 years. Overall, two-thirds of the patients (67.4%) reported significant occupational disability; 40.7% felt unable to work at all. At follow-up, the unemployment rate (38.4%) was only marginally different. However, the employment rate increased from 32.6% to 42.6%; the change was due to the fact that a substantial proportion of patients who had remained at work on a part-time basis had returned to full-time employment. Using as benchmark the fact that about 5% of adults in the U.S. claim to be unable to work (2), the study concluded that there is considerable work disability among individuals with CFS. Similar data were reported in a study of an Australian cohort (3). The average age was 34 years, and most patients were included in the range 25 to 54 years of age, which corresponded to an average adjusted unemployment rate in Australia of 12% for men and 39% for women. Before CFS, 27% of male patients and 48% of female patients had been unemployed. CFS produced an unemployment rate of 64% for men and 81% for women; the net increases were similar for males (37%) and females (34%).

[Haworth co-indexing entry note]: "Disability Evaluation for Chronic Fatigue Syndrome." Manu, Peter. Co-published simultaneously in *Journal of Chronic Fatigue Syndrome* (The Haworth Medical Press, an imprint of The Haworth Press, Inc.) Vol. 3, No. 4, 1997, pp. 9-17; and: *Disability and Chronic Fatigue Syndrome: Clinical, Legal and Patient Perspectives* (ed: Nancy G. Klimas, and Roberto Patarca) The Haworth Medical Press, an imprint of The Haworth Press, Inc., 1997, pp. 9-17. Single or multiple copies of this article are available for a fee from The Haworth Document Delivery Service [1-800-342-9678, 9:00 a.m. - 5:00 p.m. (EST). E-mail address: getinfo@haworth.com].

What are the challenges created by the disability claims of patients with CFS? The conundrum centers around the need to confirm the patient's perception of disability caused by a clinical condition defined almost exclusively in subjective terms. Most of the time, the primary care physician supports the claim of disability by finding that the patient fulfills the diagnostic criteria for the condition and by noting the persistence of subjective reports of symptoms that may affect the patient's work potential. Invariably, the disabling symptoms are cognitive deficits, exercise intolerance and pain. These symptoms lead to a number of major issues in determining the patients' ability to function. First, the subjective nature of these complaints raises the possibility of a discrepancy between self-reported and observed disability (4). Second, given the well-established association between psychiatric disorders and CFS, the possibility of psychopharmacologic improvement must be given careful consideration. Third, benefits-granting agencies are entitled to require that the principal disabling symptoms (cognitive deficits and exercise intolerance) be quantified through scientifically valid and reproducible testing. Fourth, the contribution of pain to the maintenance of the alleged disability must be carefully addressed, in a manner consistent with the American Medical Association's position that "chronic pain and pain behaviors are not, per se, impairments, but they should trigger assessments with regard to ability to function and carry out daily activities" (5). Fifth, the patients and their physicians, as well as the adjudicators for Social Security Administration and private insurance carriers, need to be able to rely on a standardized evaluation protocol for the initial and subsequent evaluations of the work ability.

1. THE DISCREPANCY BETWEEN SELF-REPORTED AND OBSERVED DISABILITY

Empirical research addressing this question has found a striking discordance between *self-assessed* and *observed* functional disability in patients with fibromyalgia, a condition sharing many clinical characteristics with CFS (6). The study compared patients given the diagnosis of fibromyalgia with age and gender matched patients diagnosed to have rheumatoid arthritis and to healthy control subjects. Six occupational therapists and 6 physicians with expertise in assessing disabilities participated as observers in the study. Observers were not told about the inclusion of the healthy control subjects.

Patients with fibromyalgia and rheumatoid arthritis completed a questionnaire on disability to rate on visual analog scales their ability to perform the following 7 activities. Five days after the self-reports the patients and the healthy control subjects actually performed the 7 activities and were recorded on videotape. The videotapes were then assessed in random order by each of the 12 observers individually. Just like the patients, observers recorded their assessment of functional disability on visual analog scales.

All observers assessed the healthy control subjects as having no evidence whatsoever of disability. Compared to observers, the patients judged themselves significantly more disabled on all 7 activities. Overall, the patients' self-reported disability was more than twice that noted by the independent observers. In contrast, for rheumatoid arthritis the discrepancy between self-report and observed scores reached statistical significance for only one activity.

2. ASSESSING THE ROLE OF PSYCHIATRIC DISORDERS IN ILLNESS AND DISABILITY MAINTENANCE

The magnitude of the psychiatric morbidity of CFS patients receiving disability benefits can be easily demonstrated. In our experience with 92 consecutive successful CFS disability claims, 79% of patients had sufficient symptomatic evidence for at least one current psychiatric disorder. The findings support data recently collected in Australia showing that among CFS patients there is a statistically homogenous subgroup characterized by more disability and a higher current psychiatric morbidity (7), underscoring the fact that a competent psychiatric evaluation is necessary in all cases in which these illnesses show an unfavorable progression or when the patients are claiming total disability.

3. SPECIALIZED TESTING TO DOCUMENT THE PRESENCE AND SEVERITY OF ALLEGED COGNITIVE DEFICITS AND EXERCISE INTOLERANCE

a. Evaluation of Cognitive Ability

Neuropsychological disturbances, particularly poor memory and difficulty with tasks that require sustained attention and concentration, are commonly reported among the disabling symptoms of patients with CFS (8). The essential tools for the assessment of cognitive ability are included in standardized batteries of neuropsychological tests. Because of its use in clinical practice and litigation, primarily for the diagnosis of dementing illnesses and adjudication of claims following traumatic closed-head injuries, neuropsychological testing is widely available, has high reliability for deficit detection and allows the assessment of motivation to perform poorly, an important issue given the effect of financial incentives on symptoms and disability (9).

The field experience supports the use of neuropsychological testing for the evaluation of disability, as shown by a recent publication describing the cognitive deficits of disabled CFS patients (10). The 29 patients included in the study were recurrently homebound or bedridden and unable to work full-time. Their mean age was 39.6 years, and they had an average of 14.3 years of education and an average duration of illness of 5.7 years. An age and gender matched control group comprised 25 healthy subjects with an average of 16.3 years of education. Patients and control subjects were administered a battery of standardized neuropsychological tests and a battery of tasks adapted for administration by computer to better measure speed and accuracy of response. The primary differences between patients and control subjects were found on test of memory and learning. Immediate recall was the function clearly impaired, as demonstrated by significant differences on the Wechsler Memory Scale (11), a word list learning task and a pattern memory task. Other domains significantly impaired were those of language, spatial ability and set shifting/conceptualization. The differences retained their significance when the degree of psychiatric symptomatology and psychoactive treatments were covaried, thus reinforcing the clinical validity of these assessments for the evaluation of disability claimed by CFS sufferers.

b. Evaluation of Exercise Tolerance

Exercise tolerance is the result of combined normal performance of the respiratory, cardiovascular and musculoskeletal systems. The method of testing consists of an integrated cardiopulmonary exercise study protocol which confirms the presence of the alleged impairment, quantifies its severity and pinpoints the system responsible (12).

Prior to testing, a history and physical examination, a resting electrocardiogram, a chest radiograph and a spirometric evaluation of pulmonary function are obtained. In general, the testing uses a limited exercise protocol to evaluate the functional status during four stages: rest, constant low intensity exercise (e.g., 3-4 minutes of treadmill walking at zero grade inclination), incremental exercise to tolerance (7-10 minutes during which the grade of incline is increased 1 to 3% every minute), and recovery. Data collected during the exercise testing of disability claimants is compared with the normative values for a sedentary working population, with appropriate corrections for age, gender and body height (12).

The main variable measured during integrated exercise testing is the *oxygen uptake,* measured in L/min or ml/min/kg. The measurement reflects the fitness of the cardiovascular system and the size of the muscle mass involved in the task. The goal is to determine the level of effort at which the blood pressure, heart rate, ventilation and output of carbon dioxide are maintained constant without increasing the oxygen debt or producing lactic acidosis. An important measure is the *lactic acidosis threshold,* because levels of effort that produce lactic acidosis require rest periods for recovery. In a normal person, the onset of lactic acidosis occurs when the individual reaches 45-60% of his peak oxygen uptake. A lactic acidosis threshold that occurs at less than 40% of the predicted peak of oxygen uptake is abnormal and reflects circulatory dysfunction or deconditioning.

In addition to documenting poor exercise tolerance, the integrated cardiopulmonary exercise testing is extremely useful in defining its possible cause. Abnormalities of the *heart, pulmonary vasculature and peripheral small vessels* have already been mentioned. Moreover, testing is useful in assessing the work intolerance created by *obesity* (increased oxygen uptake requirements at all work levels), *obstructive lung disease, restrictive lung disease, anemia, cigarette smoking, adrenergic blockade* and *defects in bioenergetics* (muscle pain during maximal exercise without elevation of blood lactate values). Of great importance is the ability of the integrated testing to detect *poor effort* in situations in which the disability claimant had stopped exercise. The finding of a low peak oxygen uptake, a high heart rate reserve, a high breathing reserve and a normal lactic acidosis threshold are among the variables indicating that the claimant has not performed at his true potential. Such testing protocols can be safely employed for patients with chronic fatigue syndrome; despite a low fitness level, a CFS cohort demonstrated the ability to withstand a maximal treadmill exercise test without a major exacerbation of either fatigue or other symptoms of their illness (13).

A study published in the current issue of *JCFS* has confirmed the value of integrated cardiopulmonary testing in assessing the functional capacity of CFS patients (14). The investigation compared the muscle function and exercise tolerance of CFS patients with those of appropriate age- and gender-matched control groups, i.e., healthy subjects and patients with a primary diagnosis of mood disorder. Isokinetic testing indicated that the fatigability, endurance and recovery of the elbow and knee muscles of CFS patients were similar to the values observed in the control subjects. However, the results of the integrated exercise testing showed that chronic fatigue syndrome patients had significant reduction in the maximal work and oxygen consumption as compared to healthy control subjects or depressed patients.

4. ASSESSING THE ROLE OF CHRONIC PAIN IN THE INITIATION AND MAINTENANCE OF DISABILITY

Most disability rating systems in the United States, including those used or proposed by the Social Security Administration, Veterans Administration and American Medical Association, take the consistent position that chronic pain cannot be considered impairment or the cause of impairment (15). Nevertheless, an attempt to measure pain must be part of disability evaluation when the symptom is considered disabling by the claimant. A number of self-reporting instruments have been developed to assess pain severity and its associated symptoms and consequences (15). For example, the West Haven-Yale Multidimensional Pain Inventory (16) evaluates the patient's ability to participate in common daily activities and the responses of others to the patient's communication of pain, the Vanderbilt Pain Management Inventory (17) evaluates patient's style of coping with pain, and the McGill Pain Questionnaire (18) measures the intensity and the affective and sensory components of the pain experience. An important task for the evaluator of disability is to determine whether the allegedly disabling chronic *pain symptom* belongs to a functional somatic syndrome (CFS or fibromyalgia) or is the defining complaint of a discrete chronic *pain syndrome*. Patients with chronic pain syndrome have an intense preoccupation with pain (not tiredness or cognitive difficulty), use pain as a symbolic means of communication, show passivity, have strong dependency needs, and are usually unable to deal appropriately with anger and hostility. Their developmental history is remarkable for emotional neglect, high incidence of alcoholism in the family, childhood trauma and early adult responsibilities (15); these characteristics have not been identified among patients with CFS and fibromyalgia. Extreme caution in making a diagnosis of disabling CFS or fibromyalgia is appropriate when the claimant has had multiple pain-related surgeries without beneficial results, is involved in pain-related litigation (workers' compensation or personal injury), has known or highly suspected major psychopathology and has a history of overuse of health care services (15). In these cases, the primary care physician should arrange a multidisciplinary evaluation in a specialized pain center.

5. THE NEED FOR STANDARDIZED PROTOCOLS FOR THE ASSESSMENT OF CLAIMS

The determination that the claimant qualifies for total disability status as a result of CFS should therefore answer the following four questions: Does the claimant have CFS? Have common comorbid psychiatric disorders been carefully evaluated and treated by a psychiatrist? Is there objective evidence of significant cognitive impairment? Is there objective evidence of critical reduction of physical strength and endurance? The research literature justifying this conceptual framework is described in a separate paper in this publication (19). For our study cohort, now enlarged to 92 claimants, the data indicated that no case had been fully assessed and that one in three patients (34%) fulfilled none of the four criteria. A substantial number (36%) of patients did not satisfy the standard definition of CFS, because of specified exclusionary clauses or insufficient symptoms. Only 33% of patients had been referred for psychiatric evaluation. Despite the fact that all patients claimed total disability on the basis of exercise intolerance and cognitive deficits, only 14% had their strength and endurance objectively measured and only 13% underwent neuropsychological testing. These data are similar to the experience published with regard to a cohort of 111 patients with chronic low-back pain; only 12% were found to have evidence of significant objective impairments (20).

In summary, the scientific evidence and clinical experience support a paradigmatic shift in the evaluation of disability of patients with CFS. This evaluation should and can become a standardized, quality-controllable, sequential process whose steps must include adequate documentation of diagnosis, careful evaluation and treatment of comorbid psychiatric disorders, objective neuropsychological and exercise tolerance testing, and thorough assessment of pain severity and its impact upon daily activities.

Peter Manu, MD, FACP
Director of Medical Services
Hillside Hospital
Long Island Jewish Medical Center
Glen Oaks, NY
and
Associate Professor of Medicine and Psychiatry
Albert Einstein College of Medicine
Bronx, NY

REFERENCES

1. Bombardier CH, Buchwald D. Chronic fatigue, chronic fatigue syndrome, and fibromyalgia. Disability and health-care use. *Medical Care* 1996;34:924-930.

2. Pope A, Tarlov A. *Disability in America: Toward a national agenda for prevention.* Washington, DC: National Academy Press, Institute of Medicine, 1991: 6-13.

3. Lloyd AR, Pender H. The economic impact of the chronic fatigue syndrome. *Med J Aust* 1992;157:599-601.

4. White KP, Harth M, Teasell RW. Work disability evaluation and the fibromyalgia syndrome. *Semin Arthritis Rheum* 1995;24:371-381.

5. *Guides to the evaluation of permanent disability* (4th ed). Chicago: American Medical Association, 1993.

6. Hidding A, van santen M, De Klerk E, Gielen X, Boers M, Geenen R, Vlaeyen J, Kester A, van den Linden S. Comprison between self-report measures and clinical observations of functional disability in ankylosing spondylitis, rheumatoid arthritis and fibromyalgia. *J Rheumatol* 1994;21:818-823.

7. Hickie I, Lloyd A, Hadzi-Pavlovic D, Parker G, Bird K, Wakefield D. Can the chronic fatigue syndrome be defined by distinct clinical features? *Psychological Med* 1995;25:925-935.

8. Grafman J. Neuropsychological assessment of patients with chronic fatigue syndrome. In: Demitrack MA, Abbey SE, eds. *Chronic fatigue syndrome: An integrative approach to evaluation and treatment.* New York: Guilford Press, 1996: 113-129.

9. Binder LM, Rohling ML. Money matters: a meta-analytic review of the effects of financial incentives on recovery after closed-head injury. *Am J Psychiatry* 1996;153:7-10.

10. Marcel B, Komaroff AL, Fagioli L, Kornish RJ, Albert MS. Cognitive deficits in patients with chronic fatigue syndrome. *Biol Psychiatry* 1996; 40:535-541.

11. Russell EW. A multiple scoring method for the assessment of complex memory functions. *J Consul Clin Psychology* 1975;43:800-809.

12. Hansen JE, Wasserman K. Integrated cardiopulmonary exercise testing. In: Demeter SL, Andersson GBJ, Smith GM, eds. *Disability evaluation.* St. Louis: American Medical Association, Mosby-Year Book, Inc., 1996: 318-337.

13. Sisto SA, LaManca J, Cordero DL. Metabolic and cardiovascular effects of a progressive exercise test in patients with chronic fatigue syndrome. *Am J Med* 1996;100:634-640.

14. Make B, Jones JF. Impairment of patients with chronic fatigue syndrome. *J Chronic Fatigue Syndrome* 1997;3(4):43-55.

15. Aronoff GM. Pain. In: Demeter SL, Andersson GBJ, Smith GM, eds. *Disability evaluation.* St. Louis: American Medical Association, Mosby-Year Book, Inc., 1996: 529-542.

16. Kerns RD, Turk DC, Rudy TE. The West Haven-Yale Multidimensional Pain Inventory. *Pain* 1985;23:345-356.

17. Brown GK, Nicassio PM. Development of a questionnaire for the assessment of active and passive coping strategies in chronic pain patients. *Pain* 1987;31:53-64.

18. Melzack R. The McGill Pain Questionnaire. *Pain* 1975;1:277-299.

19. Manu P. Long-term disability for chronic fatigue syndrome. *J Chronic Fatigue Syndrome* 1997;3(4):19-30.

20. Strang JP. The chronic disability syndrome. In: Aronoff GM, ed. *The evaluation and treatment of chronic pain* (1st ed). Baltimore: Ruban & Schwartzenberg, 1985: 231-258.

DISABILITY EVALUATION

Long-Term Disability
for Chronic Fatigue Syndrome

Peter Manu, MD, FACP

SUMMARY. To determine the quality of medical evaluations leading to long-term disability payments for chronic fatigue syndrome (CFS) we conducted a structured cross-sectional study of 76 patients receiving such benefits for an average of 2.1 years. Most of the subjects were middle-aged, white (99%), women (87%) who had been previously employed in "white-collar" jobs (96%). In all cases the claim of disability was based on subjective reports of substantial impairment in exercise tolerance and cognitive ability. The quality of disability determinations was judged by the fulfillment of four requirements: correct CFS diagnosis, psychiatric evaluation, neuropsychological testing and physical capacity measurement. The analysis indicated that none of the claims had been fully evaluated and

Peter Manu is affiliated with Departments of Medicine and Psychiatry, Long Island Jewish Medical Center and Albert Einstein College of Medicine.

Address correspondence to: Peter Manu, Medical Services, Hillside Hospital Division, Long Island Jewish Medical Center, Glen Oaks, NY 11004.

[Haworth co-indexing entry note]: "Long-Term Disability for Chronic Fatigue Syndrome." Manu, Peter. Co-published simultaneously in *Journal of Chronic Fatigue Syndrome* (The Haworth Medical Press, an imprint of The Haworth Press, Inc.) Vol. 3, No. 4, 1997, pp. 19-30; and: *Disability and Chronic Fatigue Syndrome: Clinical, Legal and Patient Perspectives* (ed: Nancy G. Klimas, and Roberto Patarca) The Haworth Medical Press, an imprint of The Haworth Press, Inc., 1997, pp. 19-30. Single or multiple copies of this article are available for a fee from The Haworth Document Delivery Service [1-800-342-9678, 9:00 a.m. - 5:00 p.m. (EST). E-mail address: getinfo@haworth.com].

19

that in 34% of cases none of the requirements had been fulfilled. The diagnosis of CFS was incorrect in 38% of cases. The majority of claimants (84%) had active psychiatric disorders, but only 32% had been evaluated by psychiatrists. Only 14% of claimants had their physical capacity objectively assessed and only 11% had formal testing of their cognitive abilities. The data suggest that most medical evaluations resulting in disability payments for CFS are flawed as a result of the overdiagnosis of CFS, the insufficient attention given the comorbid psychiatric disorders, and the infrequent objective testing of physical capacity and cognitive function. *[Article copies available for a fee from The Haworth Document Delivery Service: 1-800-342-9678. E-mail address: getinfo@haworth.com]*

Chronic fatigue syndrome (CFS) gained legitimacy in 1988 when a case-definition was proposed by a multidisciplinary group (1) assembled by the Centers for Disease Control and Prevention (CDC) and has been the focus of intense public attention and scientific research ever since. According to the latest revision of the case-definition (2), CFS is said to be present when an individual has persistent or relapsing fatigue that is of new or definite onset, has remained unexplained after a thorough clinical evaluation, is not the result of ongoing exertion, is not substantially alleviated by rest, and produces significant reduction in previous levels of occupational and social activities. In addition, at least four of the following eight symptoms must have persisted or recurred for at least six months: substantial impairment in short-memory and concentration, sore throat, tender cervical or axillary lymph nodes, muscle pain, multijoint pain, headaches of a new type, unrefreshing sleep, and postexertional malaise lasting more than 24 hours. The definition makes clear that the CFS diagnosis cannot be substantiated by abnormalities found on physical examination and that no laboratory tests or imaging procedures are required or useful for the positive identification of CFS. However, judicious and reasonably complete testing should be used to exclude other physical diagnoses and a psychiatric evaluation or structured psychiatric interview must be performed whenever the patient's history and present symptoms indicate the possibility of a psychiatric disorder.

The etiology of CFS has not been elucidated and there are no pharmacological interventions consistently effective. Over a period greater than 2 years, the natural history of CFS appears to lead to worsening or persistent symptoms in approximately one quarter of the total number of individuals given this diagnosis (3,4). In the absence of published data regarding the total number of disability allowances and monetary awards for a primary diagnosis of CFS, we can use the mean of the CFS prevalence range of 75 to 267 per 100,000 (5) and the current minimum wage to estimate that the pool of disability claimants might include 95,000 adults in the United States and require payments exceeding one billion dollars each year. Despite its magnitude, the scientific evaluation of the process by which an individual is considered disabled as a result of CFS has never been attempted.

To design this study we started from the Social Security Administration's guide for providing medical evidence for individuals with the chronic fatigue syndrome (6). The document affirms the law's definition of disability as an inability "to do substantial gainful work activity because of a medical condition that has lasted, or can be expected to last, for at least 12 months," directs the physicians to show that the chronic fatigue syndrome exists according to medically acceptable findings, and makes clear that "symptoms alone cannot be the basis for a finding of disability." We then used a model proposed for the evaluation of cardiac functional capacity (7) to infer that the determination of disability produced by CFS must establish a causal relationship between CFS and the inability to work, demonstrate CFS-related cognitive and physical impairments using reliable techniques, and determine that the claimant has reached a critical reduction in the ability to perform work-related activities.

In order to establish a causal relationship between CFS and the alleged inability to work two steps are required. The first is to scrupulously insure that the claimant's symptoms are sufficient for the diagnosis of CFS and that a thorough medical work-up excluded other conditions that produce a similar clinical picture, such as primary sleep disorders, degenerative neurologic disorders, collagen-vascular syndromes and chronic infections (2). The second is to obtain a careful psychiatric examination to determine whether the patient has a condition known to exclude the CFS diagnosis, namely any past or current diagnosis of major depression with psychotic or melancholic features, bipolar affective disorder, schizophrenia, delusional disorder, dementia, anorexia or bulimia nervosa, and substance abuse within 2 years before the onset of fatigue and at any time afterwards (2). The psychiatric evaluation should also be seen as instrumental in diagnosing and planning the therapeutic approach to conditions often seen in comorbid association with CFS, such as nonmelancholic depression, panic disorder and somatization disorder (8-11).

The demonstration of CFS-related abnormalities in the cognitive functioning is possible using standard techniques. Performed by specialized personnel with post-doctoral training, the neuropsychological evaluation offers objective measures of the information processing speed, attention, language, perception, reasoning and problem-solving, sensory function and motor coordination of patients with CFS (12-14). Similarly, physical performance assessments of CFS patients are reliably provided by exercise physiologists and occupational therapists with formal training in testing isometric and dynamic strength, exercise endurance and cardiopulmonary fitness (15-17). The cognitive and physical performance data can be used to delineate the residual functional capacity and to match it against the job-specific requirements.

The determination that the claimant qualifies for total disability status as a result of CFS must therefore answer the following four questions: (1) Does the claimant have CFS? (2) Have common comorbid psychiatric disorders been carefully evaluated and aggressively treated by a specialist? (3) Is there objective evidence of significant cognitive impairment? and (4) Is there objective evidence of critical impairment in physical strength and endurance?

These four questions were used to evaluate 76 successful claims for total disability benefits for a primary diagnosis of CFS. Because it is the first of its kind, the aim of this observational study was to assess the situation in the field, rather than test a specific hypothesis.

METHODS

Data Collection

The review of 76 total disability claims for a primary diagnosis of CFS was performed as an independent expert medical assessment during a two-year period starting in August 1994. At the initiative of five large insurance companies, claims were sent for an evaluation intended to confirm the diagnosis of CFS and to establish whether the claimant's condition qualified as total disability. The selection of cases submitted for review was entirely at the discretion of the referring insurance company. The documentation provided consisted of (1) job description, (2) employment history, (3) statements from the claimant's attending physician(s) supporting the claim for long-term disability, (4) office notes from physicians and other health care professionals involved in the claimant's care, (5) results of laboratory testing and other investigations performed for diagnostic purposes or to document the presence and severity of the claimed disability and (6) statements from claimants regarding their symptoms and their impact on their daily life and activities.

The review of each claim was conducted according to a structured protocol that was designed to establish first that the claimant had an illness characterized by a chief complaint of fatigue for at least 6 months, that a sufficiently thorough medical evaluation of the cause of the fatigue had been performed, that the illness was not attributable to a standard medical diagnosis other than CFS, and that the patient's persistent fatigue was accompanied by the symptoms required for the diagnosis of CFS. Second, statements provided by patient and physician(s) were scrutinized for the presence of symptoms suggestive of psychiatric disorders, for established psychiatric diagnoses, for referrals to psychiatrists or other mental health workers, and for treatments with psychoactive drugs or psychotherapy. Third, the record was searched for evidence that neuropsychological testing and an objective evaluation of strength and endurance had been performed. Whenever necessary, the attending physicians were contacted directly to clarify statements and to fill in missing data.

Evaluation Score

The quality of evaluation was quantitated by assigning one point each for (1) correct CFS diagnosis, (2) psychiatric consultation, (3) objective evaluation of muscle strength and physical endurance, and (4) standardized neuropsychological testing. Therefore, each case received a global evaluation score theoretically ranging from 0 (worst) to 4 (best).

Statistical Analysis

A one-way analysis of variance was used to test the correlation between the evaluation scores and the characteristics of the patients and their physicians. Confidence intervals for proportions were calculated according to the standard formula (18).

RESULTS

Physicians' Characteristics

Most of the physicians in charge of these 76 patients were trained in internal medicine (53%) or family practice (21%). In the remainder of the cases, the patients were under the care of a psychiatrist (8%) or other specialty physicians (18%). In some instances the physician's specialty was highly unusual for a condition with the clinical complexity of CFS. For example, pediatricians were in charge for patients 40 and 47 years of age; a pathologist requested disability benefits for a diagnosis of "CFS secondary to Epstein-Barr virus" in a patient with major depression and panic disorder; an ear, nose and throat specialist supported the claim of total disability for a diagnosis of "CFS and Candida-related complex" in a patient with dysthymia and substance use disorder.

The majority (74%) of physicians expressed strong convictions with regard to the etiology of CFS. The most commonly held beliefs were that CFS was produced by an immune dysfunction (41% of physicians), a viral infection (26%) or other physical cause (7%).

Patients' Demographic and Occupational Characteristics

Of the 76 patients, 66 were women (87%) and 75 were white (99%); the average age was 39.9 years (standard deviation 8.2 years). The patients had been receiving disability benefits for an average of 2.1 years (standard deviation 1.9 years). The majority of patients had worked in managerial positions (29%), clerical (27%) and sales (15%) jobs. Other traditional "white collar" occupations included teachers, attorneys, writers and engineers (for a cumulative 14%) and nurses (5%). Only 3 patients (4%) had been employed in "blue collar" jobs.

Medical Diagnoses

Five (7%) patients had clinical and laboratory evidence of physical disorders sufficient to explain their chronic fatigue illness. The diagnoses were hypothyroidism, multiple sclerosis, obstructive sleep apnea, metastatic ovarian adenocarcinoma and morbid obesity.

Psychiatric Diagnoses

Sixty-two (84%) patients had been given or had sufficient symptomatic evidence for at least one current psychiatric diagnosis (Table 1). Two-thirds (67%) of patients had either major depression or dysthymia, i.e., mood disorders characterized by substantial and prolonged fatigue.

Therapeutic Intervention

Although 82% of claimants had active mood disorders, only 68% had been treated with antidepressant drugs; 59% were receiving serotonin re-uptake inhibitors (usually fluoxetine or sertraline) and 9% were taking

TABLE 1. Current Psychiatric Disorders

	Pts.	%	95% CI
Patients With Psychiatric Disorders	64	84	76-92
Mood Disorders	62	82	73-91
Major Depression	48	63	52-74
Dysthymia	4	5	0-10
Bipolar Disorder	2	3	0-7
Depressive Disorders NOS	8	11	4-18
Anxiety Disorders	20	26	16-36
Panic Disorder	13	17	9-25
Generalized Anxiety Disorder	3	4	0-8
Post-traumatic Stress Disorder	3	4	0-8
Anxiety Disorder NOS	1	1	0-3
Somatoform Disorders	17	22	13-31
Somatization Disorder	12	16	8-24
Conversion Disorder	4	5	0-10
Hypochondriasis	1	1	0-3
Substance Use Disorders	4	5	0-10
Dissociative Disorders	2	3	0-7
Patients Without Psychiatric Disorders	12	16	8-24

NOS = Not Otherwise Specified; CI = Confidence Interval

tricyclic agents (usually amitryptiline or nortryptyline). The dosages employed were generally low and had been infrequently adjusted upward for increased efficacy. The second most common class of drugs (38% of patients) were high-potency anxiolytic benzodiazepines (alprazolam and clonazepam). In contrast with the antidepressant drugs, which appeared to be underutilized, benzodiazepines were overutilized in this population with a 21% rate of benzodiazepine-responsive anxiety disorders.

Other therapeutic interventions included rest (65% of patients), pain medications (20%) and the administration by injection of porcine liver extracts (20%) and gammaglobulin (17%). More than half of the patients (52%) had been taking large doses of vitamins and mineral supplements as recommended by their physicians.

Alternative medical practices (e.g., intravenous vitamin infusions, colon irrigation, acupuncture, "yeast-free" diet) had been tried by 38% of the patients studied.

Quality of Disability Evaluations

The evaluation scores indicated that the overall quality of these disability determinations was poor. None of the cases had been fully assessed and one-third of the patients did not satisfy even one of the four criteria (Table 2).

The degree to which the specific evaluation criteria were met is presented in Table 3. A substantial number of patients (38%) did not satisfy the standard diagnostic definition of CFS (2). One example is that of a middle-aged female patient with 14 psychiatric hospitalizations in the past 5 years for major depression with psychotic features and multiple personality disorder. The CFS definition is clear in excluding patients with psychotic depression. Another example is that of a middle-aged female with a history of cocaine dependence who was diagnosed to have CFS within six months after cocaine detoxification. The CFS definition excludes patients with substance abuse within two years before the onset of fatigue. A third example is that of middle-aged female patient whose recorded weight ranged from 148 kg to 156 kg during the year prior to the CFS diagnosis; the patient's height was 1.66 meters. The patient's weight and height

TABLE 2. Quality of Disability Evaluations

Evaluation Score	Pts.	%	95% CI
0 (worst)	26	34	23-45
1	38	50	39-61
2	10	13	5-21
3	2	3	0-7
4 (best)	0	0	0

CI = Confidence Interval

TABLE 3. Requirements of Disability Evaluations

Requirement Fulfilled	Pts.	%	95% CI
CFS Diagnostic Criteria	47	62	51-73
Psychiatric Consultation	24	32	22-42
Strength/Endurance Testing	11	14	7-21
Neuropsychological Testing	8	11	4-18

CI = Confidence Interval

computed a body mass index of 55, well above the limit considered exclusionary by the CFS definition.

All patients claimed total disability on the basis of cognitive deficits and exercise intolerance, but only 1 in 7 (14%) had their strength and endurance quantitated and only 1 in 8 (11%) underwent neuropsychological testing.

The results of the one-way analysis of variance indicated that the likelihood of a poor evaluation increased when the patient was a woman ($p = 0.02$) who had been prescribed vitamins ($p = 0.03$) by a physician whose specialty was not internal medicine ($p = 0.09$).

DISCUSSION

Patients with CFS create significant problems for private and public institutions that adjudicate claims for total disability because the condition is defined exclusively in subjective terms. The complete reliance on symptoms reported by individuals with generally normal findings on physical examination stands in contrast to the main goal of a process meant to identify and measure the dysfunction that prevents the continuation of employment. The importance of the issue has been recognized in 1992 and 1994 at the last two national meetings of the American Association for Chronic Fatigue Syndrome, large forums which included researchers, clinicians and patients. The position statements made at these meetings recommended "tests of short-term of sustained activity, motor strength, stamina, and neurocognitive function" (19) and indicated that "cardiopulmonary exercise testing will aid CFS patients in qualifying for disability" (20), "psychometric testing is obtained to document the presence and severity of neurocognitive losses" and "psychiatric evaluation when the evidence points to the presence of an anxiety or mood disorder" (21).

Our data suggest that the message has not been heard and that total disability for CFS is often granted to individuals who do not meet criteria for this diagnosis, have psychiatric disorders insufficiently recognized and inexpertly treated, and have never been tested for objective evidence of impairment in their exercise ability and cognitive functioning.

The study identified a striking predominance of women and a high prevalence of psychiatric disorders among this group of patients with chronic fatigue. The findings support data recently collected in Australia showing that among the patients currently diagnosed with CFS there is a 27% statistically homogenous subgroup characterized by more disability, greater proportion of females, higher current psychiatric morbidity, more symptoms and more hypochondriacal concerns (4). Similar findings were reported in a study of symptom persistence at 2 1/2-years after initial evaluation of chronic fatigue patients in Seattle (3). The patients showing no recovery had a significantly higher prevalence of lifetime major depression, dysthymia, generalized anxiety disorder and somatization disorder, as well as more somatic symptoms. This degree of agreement between three different populations underscores the fact that a competent psychiatric evaluation is necessary in all cases in which fatigue illnesses have an unfavorable progression, including, of course, all patients claiming total disability for CFS.

The finding that only 11% of our study group had been sent for neuropsychological testing of their cognitive function is difficult to explain given the fact that poor memory and difficulty with attention and concentration were mentioned as disabling symptoms by all the claimants in our study group. Because of its use in litigation, primarily for traumatic closed-head injuries, neuropsychological testing is widely available, has high reliability for deficit detection and allows the assessment of motivation to perform poorly, an important issue given the effect of financial incentives on symptoms and disability (22). Among well-defined CFS patients, recent data indicates no impairment on tests of memory relative to controls, a finding which was in stark contrast to the fact that these patients had the highest degree of subjective complaints of cognitive impairments (14). The same authors also established that despite their fatigue, depression and anxiety, CFS patients can perform higher level cognitive tasks at the level of healthy subjects, an encouraging notion given the fact that managers were the largest group among our study population.

Our review also highlighted the paucity of objective data regarding exercise tolerance among our group of patients claiming total disability as a result of muscle weakness, easy fatigability after mild exertion and prolonged post-exercise malaise. Despite the fact that such symptoms are reported by all CFS patients, recent data have shown that they perform within the normal range of oxidative capacity and that they could withstand a maximal treadmill exercise test without a substantial exacerbation in either fatigue or other symptoms of their condition (17).

The issues brought to light by this cross-sectional observational study are important and should stimulate larger prospective investigations of the objective evidence of disability among those who have left the workforce because of chronic fatigue. For now, however, we feel that the field realities and an abundance of basic research data form the basis of rational process for the determination of disability in CFS. This should include a thorough internal medicine evaluation to rule out physical causes of fatigue followed by a comprehensive psychiatric evaluation. The finding of current psychiatric diagnoses must lead to aggressive psychopharmacological and cognitive-behavioral interventions. If symptoms persist, the residual functional capacity will have to be objectively assessed through neuropsychological and exercise testing and the results interpreted in light of the specific job requirements.

REFERENCES

1. Holmes GP, Kaplan JE, Gantz NM, et al. Chronic fatigue syndrome: a working case definition. *Ann Intern Med* 1988;108:387-9.

2. Fukuda K, Straus SE, Hickie I, et al. The chronic fatigue syndrome: a comprehensive approach to its definition and study. *Ann Intern Med* 1994;121:953-9.

3. Clark MR, Katon W, Russo J, et al. Chronic fatigue: risk factors for symptoms persistence in a 2 1/2-year follow-up study. *Am J Med* 1995;98:187-195.

4. Hickie I, Lloyd A, Hadzi-Pavlovic D, et al. Can the chronic fatigue syndrome be defined by distinct clinical features? *Psychological Med* 1995;25:925-35.

5. Buchwald D, Umali P, Umali J, et al. Chronic fatigue and the chronic fatigue syndrome: prevalence in a Pacific Northwest health care system. *Ann Intern Med* 1995;123:81-88.

6. Social Security Administration. Providing medical evidence to the Social Security Administration for individuals with chronic fatigue syndrome: a guide for health professionals. *SSA Publication* 64-063.

7. Wenger NH. Ability, disability, and the functional capacity of patients with cardiovascular disease. *Trans Assoc Life Insur Med Dir Am* 1991;74:78-91.

8. Kruesi MJP, Dale J, Straus SE. Psychiatric diagnoses in patients who have chronic fatigue syndrome. *J Clin Psychiatry* 1989;50:53-6.

9. Katon W, Buchwald D, Simon G, et al. Psychiatric illness in patients with chronic fatigue and rheumatoid arthritis. *J Gen Intern Med* 1991;6:277-85.

10. Lane TJ, Manu P, Matthews DA. Depression and somatization in the chronic fatigue syndrome. *Am J Med* 1991;91:335-344.

11. Wessely S, Chalder T, Hirsch S, et al. Psychological symptoms, somatic symptoms, and psychiatric disorder in chronic fatigue and chronic fatigue syn-

drome: a prospective study in the primary care setting. *Am J Psychiatry* 1996;153:1050-9.

12. Sandman CA, Barron JL, Nackoul K, et al. Memory deficits associated with chronic fatigue immune dysfunction syndrome. *Biol Psychiatry* 1993;33: 618-23.

13. Grafman J, Schwartz V, Dale JK, et al. Analysis of neuropsychological functioning in patients with chronic fatigue syndrome. *J Neurol Neurosurg Psychiatry* 1993;56:684-9.

14. DeLuca J, Johnson SK, Beldowicz D, et al. Neuropsychological impairment in chronic fatigue syndrome, multiple sclerosis, and depression. *J Neurol Neurosurg Psychiatry* 1995;58:34-43.

15. Riley MS, O'Brien CJ, McCluskey DR, et al. Aerobic work capacity in patients with chronic fatigue syndrome. *BMJ* 1990;301:953-6.

16. Maffulli N, Testa V, Capasso G. Post-viral syndrome: a longitudinal assessment in varsity athletes. *J Sports Med Phys Fitness* 1993;33:392-9.

17. Sisto SA, LaManca J, Cordero DL, et al. Metabolic and cardiovascular effects of a progressive exercise tests in patients with chronic fatigue syndrome. *Am J Med* 1996;100:634-40.

18. Gardner MJ, Altman DG. Confidence intervals rather than P values: estimation rather than hypothesis testing. *BMJ* 1986:746-50.

19. Loveless MO, Lloyd A, Perpich R. Summary of public policy and chronic fatigue syndrome: a perspective. *Clin Inf Dis* 1994;18(Suppl 1):S163-5.

20. Stevens SR. Using exercise testing to document functional disability in CFS. *JCFS* 1995;1:127-9.

21. Harrison AL. Development and evaluation of claims involving chronic fatigue syndrome (CFS) under the Social Security disability provisions. *JCFS* 1995;1:131-3.

22. Binder LM, Rohling ML. Money matters: a meta-analytic review of the effects of financial incentives on recovery after closed-head injury. *Am J Psychiatry* 1996;153:7-10.

Neuropsychological Assessment of Chronic Fatigue Syndrome

Mariana Dimitrov, PhD
Jordan Grafman, PhD

One of the cardinal complaints of patients with chronic fatigue syndrome (CFS) is impaired cognition. Between 50% and 86% of CFS patients in published studies claim that their cognitive functioning is impaired (1,2). Most patients define these cognitive complaints as the ones causing them the greatest frustration and disability. Neuropsychological testing, therefore, plays an increasingly important role in the assessment of CFS, as well as in developing a working definition of the disease.

Neuropsychological evaluations are an integral part of the clinical neuroscience workup of most patients with neurological and psychiatric disorders. Neuropsychological evaluations provide the referral source with clinical and quantitative information about the patients' cognitive processes and mood state. The standard neuropsychological evaluation typically examines motor coordination and strength, simple sensory functions, general intellectual functioning, information processing speed, attention, language, perception, reasoning and problem-solving, memory, mood state and personality. The neuropsychological evaluation, in conjunction with subjective measures of functional ability, is the premier way to determine cognitive

Mariana Dimitrov and Jordan Grafman are affiliated with Cognitive Neuroscience Section, MNB/NINDS/NIH.

Address correspondence to: Jordan Grafman, Cognitive Neuroscience Section, NIH/NINDS/MNB, Building 10; Room 5S209, 10 Center Drive; MSC 1440, Bethesda, MD 20892-1440. E-Mail: jgr@box-j.nih.gov

[Haworth co-indexing entry note]: "Neuropsychological Assessment of Chronic Fatigue Syndrome." Dimitrov, Mariana, and Jordan Grafman. Co-published simultaneously in *Journal of Chronic Fatigue Syndrome* (The Haworth Medical Press, an imprint of The Haworth Press, Inc.) Vol. 3, No. 4, 1997, pp. 31-42; and: *Disability and Chronic Fatigue Syndrome: Clinical, Legal and Patient Perspectives* (ed: Nancy G. Klimas, and Roberto Patarca) The Haworth Medical Press, an imprint of The Haworth Press, Inc., 1997, pp. 31-42. Single or multiple copies of this article are available for a fee from The Haworth Document Delivery Service [1-800-342-9678, 9:00 a.m. - 5:00 p.m. (EST). E-mail address: getinfo@haworth.com].

ability and disability. In addition, when job-specific requirements are taken into consideration, then performance on neuropsychological tests tailored to mimic job-specific cognitive requirements can be significantly correlated with specific aspects of job performance. Subject motivation can affect performance on neuropsychological tests, but experienced neuropsychologists will be able to interpret the subject pattern of performance across many measures in the context of a subject's motivation.

The neuropsychological evaluation of CFS patients can be useful as an aid in interpreting their neurological complaints, in estimating symptom progression or rate of patient recovery, and in proposing appropriate therapies (3-5). It is particularly important when a diagnosis is one of exclusion, as it is with CFS, to establish a neuropsychological baseline by which subsequent clinical fluctuation could be judged.

SUMMARY OF NEUROPSYCHOLOGICAL STUDIES

Over the past several years, researchers have tried to objectively quantify the nature and extent of the cognitive difficulties experienced by patients with CFS. In summarizing the results from the growing body of neuropsychological studies so far published, a few general observations can be made, despite the differences in subject selection, methodology, and test batteries used across these studies.

A majority of CFS patients will have marked *complaints* of cognitive deficits particularly in the domains of memory, attention and concentration, speed of processing and problem solving (3,6-9). A majority of patients will also have marked *complaints* of emotional distress (4,8). In some studies, the severity of the cognitive and mood-state complaints tend to be correlated.

Objective neuropsychological testing does not substantiate the severity of the cognitive complaints of CFS patients. A consistent finding across studies is the discrepancy between objective performance and subjective reports of cognitive deficits. There are studies in which no relation between objective test results and subjective complaints has been found (7,10-12). However, some areas of cognitive deficit emerge from objective testing, the most frequently identified of them being in the domains of memory, attention, and information processing speed. The severity of the objectively recorded cognitive deficits varies, although most deficits fall into the borderline to mild range. In some instances, adjustment for level of psychopathology removed the existing between-group differences in cognitive performance.

Several studies report worse performance of CFS patients on memory tests compared with normal control subjects (6,8,9,13-15). There is some evidence that CFS patients have more difficulty remembering well-structured as opposed to loosely structured information (8). CFS patients have also shown some impairments on verbal memory tasks which require more effort, such as retrieval of self-ordered responses and memorizing of semantically unrelated word pairs (14). CFS patients appear to benefit less from cueing and context than controls on paired associate learning and story memory tests (6,9,16,17) and perform worse on semantic memory tasks (18,19), although there are studies with no significant differences found between CFS patients and controls on paired associates (11,13) or semantic memory tests (9,16). Mild memory impairments on tasks requiring conceptually driven encoding and retrieval processes were found by Grafman et al. (1993). Composite general memory scores on the California verbal learning test (CVLT) and the Wechsler memory scale (WMS) were within the normal range and not significantly different from those of controls as reported by several investigators (7,11,16,17,20,21). However, other investigators have identified some differences between the scores of CFS patients and controls on certain measures of the CVLT and WMS (6,9,13,17,22). DeLuca et al. (1995) suggested that slowness in information processing in the CFS group, which limits elaboration of information during encoding, could explain some of the memory deficits demonstrated by CFS patients. Despite the above-mentioned examples of CFS patient memory deficits, no consistent or severe memory impairment is evident from the performance of patients with CFS on neuropsychological tests (23).

In the domain of attention, there are several studies reporting normal performance of CFS patients on tasks of concentration and visual attention such as the trail making test, the embedded figures test, cancellation tasks and the digit symbol subtest of WAIS-R (9,13,19,20,22,24). Performance of CFS patients on digit span tasks measuring short-term memory and attention has been found comparable with controls (6,13,19,20,25). Some researchers report that CFS patients, in comparison to their matched controls, perform poorly on tasks of sustained divided attention (22,26). On the Stroop test, which measures visual attention and susceptibility to interference with irrelevant stimuli, CFS patients have been found to have abnormally slower reaction times for the interference condition (12,19,20,24). However, these deficits may stem from their slower information processing, which would be particularly compromising on complex cognitive tasks (23).

Higher cognitive functions such as conceptualization, planning and problem solving, generally appear intact in CFS patients. On the Wisconsin card sorting test, which measures concept formation and ability to abstract and categorize information, CFS patients' performance was comparable to normal controls and within the normal range (9,20). On other tests requiring concept formation, such as the similarities subtest of the Wechsler Adult Intelligence Scale-Revised (WAIS-R), the symbol digit test and category tests, CFS patients demonstrated unimpaired ability for verbal and non-verbal conceptualization. On a test of problem solving abilities, in which CFS patients were allowed to ask twenty questions in order to find a solution to a particular problem, their performance was as good as their matched controls (6). CFS patient planning ability has been observed to be intact on the object assembly and block design WAIS-R subtests, as well as on the Tower of Hanoi and Tower of London tests (6,11,13,20).

Measures of general intellectual functioning, such as the full scale verbal and performance IQs of the WAIS-R, the Shipley institute of living scale, and the national adult reading test, have shown no evidence of intellectual deficits in CFS patients (7,9-11).

The perceptual abilities of CFS patients were no different than normal controls as indicated by their performance on the performance scale WAIS-R subtests (11,13,20,27). Patients with CFS also performed within the normal range on the Luria-Nebraska scale which measures visual and spatial perception (16). Intact neural processing of sensory information by CFS patients has been observed (7,28).

Several authors have found delayed motor responses in CFS patients. Scheffers et al. (1992) and Prasher et al. (1990) found that while the error rates of their CFS patients on discrimination tasks were similar to those of the normal controls, the CFS patients had significantly slower reaction times. In another study, in which simple and serial reaction time tests were given to both CFS patient and normal control groups, CFS patients had slower reaction times (19). However, there are studies in which CFS patients showed normal response time and psychomotor performance (9,13,16,25). The observed slower response times to stimuli in some CFS patient studies might be related to their delayed information processing in executing motor programs (23).

CFS patients, in comparison with controls, report higher levels of fatigue and symptoms of stress during experiments. On many tests of memory and cognitive processing, however, CFS patients' performance is not sensitive to fatigue and remains stable over the time of testing as indicated by normal brain electrophysiological activity and stable response times (7,20,28,29).

MRI abnormalities are not a prominent feature of CFS, but some

SPECT abnormalities have been detected in a few studies (27,30-32). So far, no study has been able to correlate neuroimaging abnormalities with clinical findings in CFS, thus making neuroimaging studies of the brain not helpful for the diagnosis of CFS except to help exclude other diseases masquerading as CFS.

THE TARGETED NEUROPSYCHOLOGICAL ASSESSMENT

As a result of these findings, we suggest that the standard neuropsychological screening evaluation for CFS should include tasks that focus on memory, attentional processes, response times, information processing speed, and problem solving. Some attempt to estimate pre-morbid cognitive abilities would be useful, given that CFS patients are generally premorbidly bright and thus currently obtained scores that are simply compared to a normative sample may underestimate the true level of any objectively observed deficit. It is possible to estimate premorbid functioning of patients using reading tests or a composite score based on the Wechsler Adult Intelligence Scale subtests. Some personality scales measuring anxiety, depression, somatization, and level of fatigue and its effects upon interpersonal functioning should also be included. A scale that measures the cognitive complaints of CFS patients and another that records the observations of a family member should be compared with their objective test performance. A careful mood state and personality evaluation can help account for some of the confounding variables (e.g., decreased effort or diminished motivation due to a depressive disorder) which may affect performance on cognitive tasks. The addition of a psychiatric interview and scales examining premorbid psychiatric status can also aid in determining whether the patient was depressed or had another psychiatric condition preceding the onset of their chronic fatigue syndrome. Table 1 lists some of the domains and types of tests potentially useful in the examination of CFS patients. When possible, a formal psychiatric diagnostic interview should be conducted with each patient by a trained examiner. Since the patient may have cycles of fatigue, testing can be scheduled to optimize test performance or to assess the patient when she/he is most fatigued (33).

ETIOLOGY

There are several possible explanations for the pattern of cognitive deficits noted in CFS patients. For example, CFS could involve lesions or

TABLE 1. Domains of Cognitive Functioning and Suggested Tests.

Function Tested/Suggested Tests	Description
Intelligence	
Wechsler Adult Intelligence Scale-Revised	Measures a broad range of verbal and non-verbal cognitive abilities
Reasoning, Planning and Problem Solving	
Wisconsin Card Sorting Test	Measures concept formation
Tower of Hanoi Test	Measures planning and problem solving
20 questions	Measures problem solving
Memory	
Wechsler Memory Scale-Revised	Measures a broad range of recall, recognition and orientation processes
California Verbal Learning Test	Measures verbal learning and recognition
Continuous Visual Recognition Test	Measures nonverbal recognition
Attention	
Simple and Choice Reaction Time Tasks	Measures response speed and selection
Posner Spatial Attention Task	Measures focal spatial attention
Selective Attention and Response Competition Task	Measures selective attention and response competition
Stroop Test	Measures visual attention and susceptibility to interference
Trail Making Test	Measures visual attention and concentration
Dichotic Listening Test	Measures divided attention
Paced Auditory Serial Addition Test	Measures cognitive resource allocation and task switching
Language	
Word Fluency	Measures retrieval of items from semantic memory
Mood State and Personality	
Fatigue Severity Scale	Quantitative measure of fatigue
Beck Depression Inventory	Measures number of depressive symptoms
Minnesota Multiphasic Personality Inventory	Measures symptoms of psychopathology
Spielberger State-Trait Anxiety Scale	Measures symptoms of anxiety
Psychiatric Interview	Derives a psychiatric diagnosis

dysfunction in one or more subcortical brain structures (e.g., hypothalamic-pituitary dysfunction) that are in turn partially responsible for the instantiation of the specific cognitive processes that patients complain about being impaired (e.g., memory or speed of information processing).

Fatigue and psychiatric illness can be inextricably intertwined (34). Some authors associate CFS with a preceding or concurrent psychopathologic condition, such as depression, anxiety, emotional distress, or somatization disorder (6,11,13,14,20,25,35-40). CFS, as a chronic illness, could also lead to a reactive psychiatric disorder such as depression, which would then affect the effort patients would make on specific cognitive tasks. Patients' personal beliefs about their disease might contribute to their subjective cognitive complaints (41-43). On the positive side, there are a number of studies reporting significant improvement of the patients' cognitive complaints as a result of cognitive behavioral therapy (44-49).

Stress and psychosocial vulnerability are important determinants of immune function. Therefore, the cognitive deficits in CFS could also represent an exaggerated behavioral response in certain personalities to a "normally" occurring fluctuation in neuroimmune system regulation due to increased stress induced by problems in interpersonal or professional relationships or due to a nonspecifically heightened immune response to a viral or ecological antigen (37,47,50-60).

The interaction of infection, immunity, stress, psychiatric disorder and social factors provides a complex illustration of the subtle interface between the psyche and soma (55) and suggests that an understanding of the etiology of CFS will require a multifactorial explanation.

Because of the diagnostic dilemma posed by CFS patients and the current lack of hard neurological signs, it will be an interesting challenge for neuropsychologists to interpret their test results in the context of the myriad of referral questions they receive regarding CFS patients. In addition, studying patients whose illness is characterized by a persistent fatigue (particularly in the absence of a confirmed psychiatric disorder/history) can help neuropsychologists understand the effects of peripheral and central fatigue upon the execution of specific cognitive functions, an as-yet unresolved issue in interpreting the results of a neuropsychological evaluation that can often last several hours. Finally, mild neuropsychological deficits, by themselves, are surely not proof of CNS dysfunction or lesions. Neuropsychologists must place their results in the context of the overall evaluation of the patient.

CONCLUSIONS

Chronic fatigue syndrome is a diagnostic entity that eludes a single etiologic description but is accepted as a bona fide illness by the medical community (4,52,53,61-68). Studies to date, in general, have only revealed relatively minor cognitive problems in CFS patients. These problems lie primarily in the domains of memory, processing speed, and attention. To date, studies indicate that the severity of impairment in these cognitive domains as *reported* by the CFS patients exceeds their objective performance.

Neuropsychological testing should be done in conjunction with a medical diagnostic workup which is targeted to evaluate whether the patient meets the CDC CFS criteria which currently, and unfortunately, is not strictly adhered to but instead depends on the hospital, region and country where the diagnosis is made (4,65,69).

Regardless of comparisons of CFS to neurasthenia or the words of pundits who dismiss CFS as nothing more than a "yuppie disease" or a psychiatric diagnosis, these patients present with cognitive complaints that require the involvement of trained neuropsychologists for assessment. The inclusion of a neuropsychological evaluation in the medical workup for CFS will surely lead to improved sensitivity, if not specificity, and characterization of the disabling neurological and behavioral symptoms so often reported by patients with this disorder.

REFERENCES

1. Komaroff AL. Chronic "post-infectious" fatigue syndrome. Trans Am Acad Insur Med Annu Meet 1993;76:82-95.

2. Komaroff AL, Fagioli LR, Doolittle TH, et al. Health status in patients with chronic fatigue syndrome and in general population and disease comparison groups. Am J Med 1996;101:281-290.

3. Grafman J, Johnson R, Jr., Scheffers M. Cognitive and mood-state changes in patients with chronic fatigue syndrome. Rev Infect Dis 1991;13 Suppl 1: S45-52.

4. Schluederberg A, Straus SE, Peterson P, et al. NIH conference. Chronic fatigue syndrome research. Definition and medical outcome assessment. Ann Intern Med 1992;117:325-331.

5. Vercoulen JH, Swanink CM, Fennis JF, Galama JM, van der Meer JW, Bleijenberg G. Prognosis in chronic fatigue syndrome: a prospective study on the natural course. J Neurol Neurosurg Psychiatry 1996;60:489-494.

6. Grafman J, Schwartz V, Dale JK, Scheffers M, Houser C, Straus SE. Analysis of neuropsychological functioning in patients with chronic fatigue syndrome. J Neurol Neurosurg Psychiatry 1993;56:684-689.

7. Scheffers MK, Johnson R, Jr., Grafman J, Dale JK, Straus SE. Attention and short-term memory in chronic fatigue syndrome patients: an event-related potential analysis. Neurology 1992;42:1667-1675.

8. Grafman J. Neuropsychological features of chronic fatigue syndrome. In: Straus SE, ed. Chronic fatigue syndrome. New York: Marcel Dekker, 1994: 263-283.

9. Riccio M, Thompson C, Wilson B, Morgan DJ, Lant AF. Neuropsychological and psychiatric abnormalities in myalgic encephalomyelitis: a preliminary report. Br J Clin Psychol 1992;31:111-120.

10. Altay HT, Toner BB, Brooker H, Abbey SE, Salit IE, Garfinkel PE. The neuropsychological dimensions of postinfectious neuromyasthenia (chronic fatigue syndrome): a preliminary report. Int J Psychiatry Med 1990;20:141-149.

11. Cope H, David A, Pelosi A, Mann A. Chronic fatigue syndrome [letter; comment]. Lancet 1995;345:131.

12. Ray C, Phillips L, Weir WR. Quality of attention in chronic fatigue syndrome: subjective reports of everyday attention and cognitive difficulty, and performance on tasks of focused attention. Br J Clin Psychol 1993;32:357-364.

13. Krupp LB, Sliwinski M, Masur DM, Friedberg F, Coyle PK. Cognitive functioning and depression in patients with chronic fatigue syndrome and multiple sclerosis. Arch Neurol 1994;51:705-710.

14. Joyce E, Blumenthal S, Wessely S. Memory, attention, and executive function in chronic fatigue syndrome. J Neurol Neurosurg Psychiatry 1996;60:495-503.

15. Marcel B, Komaroff AL, Fagioli LR, Kornish RJ, 2nd, Albert MS. Cognitive deficits in patients with chronic fatigue syndrome. Biol Psychiatry 1996; 40:535-541.

16. Sandman CA, Barron JL, Nackoul K, Goldstein J, Fidler F. Memory deficits associated with chronic fatigue immune dysfunction syndrome. Biol Psychiatry 1993;33:618-623.

17. Millon C, Salvato F, Blaney N, et al. A psychological assessment of chronic fatigue syndrome/chronic Epstein-Barr virus patients. Psychological Health 1989;31:31-41.(abst)

18. Smith A. Cognitive changes in myalgic encephalomyelitis. In: Jenkins R, Mowbray JF eds. Post-viral fatigue syndrome. New York: Wiley, 1991:179-194.

19. Smith A, Behan PO, Bell W, Millar K, Bakheit M. Behavioral problems associated with chronic fatigue syndrome. Br J Psychol 1993;84:411-423.(abst)

20. Schmaling KB, DiClementi JD, Cullum CM, Jones JF. Cognitive functioning in chronic fatigue syndrome and depression: a preliminary comparison. Psychosom Med 1994;56:383-388.

21. Johnson SK, Deluca J, Fiedler N, Natelson BH. Cognitive functioning of patients with chronic fatigue syndrome. Clin Infect Dis 1994;18 Suppl 1:S84-5.

22. Deluca J, Johnson SK, Beldowicz D, Natelson BH. Neuropsychological impairments in chronic fatigue syndrome, multiple sclerosis, and depression. J Neurol Neurosurg Psychiatry 1995;58:38-43.

23. Moss-Morris R, Petrie KJ, Large RG, Kydd RR. Neuropsychological deficits in chronic fatigue syndrome: artifact or reality? [editorial]. J Neurol Neurosurg Psychiatry 1996;60:474-477.

24. Brickman AL, Fins AI. Psychological and cognitive aspects of chronic fatigue syndrome. In: Goodnik PJ, Klimas NA, eds. Chronic fatigue and related immune deficiency syndrome. Washington: American Psychiatric Press, 1993:67-93.

25. McDonald E, Cope H, David A. Cognitive impairment in patients with chronic fatigue: a preliminary study [published erratum appears in J Neurol Neurosurg Psychiatry 1993 Oct;56(10):1142]. J Neurol Neurosurg Psychiatry 1993; 56:812-815.

26. Deluca J, Johnson SK, Natelson BH. Information processing efficiency in chronic fatigue syndrome and multiple sclerosis. Arch Neurol 1993;50:301-304.

27. Cope H, Pernet A, Kendall B, David A. Cognitive functioning and magnetic resonance imaging in chronic fatigue. Br J Psychiatry 1995;167:86-94.

28. Polich J, Moore AP, Wiederhold MD. P300 assessment of chronic fatigue syndrome. J Clin Neurophysiol 1995;12:186-191.

29. Wood GC, Bentall RP, Gopfert M, Dewey ME, Edwards RH. The differential response of chronic fatigue, neurotic and muscular dystrophy patients to experimental psychological stress. Psychol Med 1994;24:357-364.

30. Cope H, David AS. Neuroimaging in chronic fatigue syndrome [editorial]. J Neurol Neurosurg Psychiatry 1996;60:471-473.

31. Schwartz RB, Garada BM, Komaroff AL, et al. Detection of intracranial abnormalities in patients with chronic fatigue syndrome: comparison of MR imaging and SPECT. AJR Am J Roentgenol 1994;162:935-941.

32. Schwartz RB, Komaroff AL, Garada BM, et al. SPECT imaging of the brain: comparison of findings in patients with chronic fatigue syndrome, AIDS dementia complex, and major unipolar depression. AJR Am J Roentgenol 1994; 162:943-951.

33. Wood C, Magnello ME, Sharpe MC. Fluctuations in perceived energy and mood among patients with chronic fatigue syndrome [see comments]. J R Soc Med 1992;85:195-198.

34. Manu P, Lane TJ, Matthews DA. Chronic fatigue and chronic fatigue syndrome: clinical epidemiology and aetiological classification. Ciba Found Symp 1993;173:23-31; discussion 31-42.

35. Katon WJ, Buchwald DS, Simon GE, Russo JE, Mease PJ. Psychiatric illness in patients with chronic fatigue and those with rheumatoid arthritis [see comments]. J Gen Intern Med 1991;6:277-285.

36. Katon WJ, Walker EA. The relationship of chronic fatigue to psychiatric illness in community, primary care and tertiary care samples. Ciba Found Symp 1993;173:193-204.

37. Manu P, Lane TJ, Matthews DA. Ideopathic Chronic Fatigue, depressive symptoms and functional somatic complaints. In: Demitrack MA, Abbey SE, eds. Chronic Fatigue Syndrome–An Integrative Approach to Evaluation and Treatment. New York: The Guilford Press, 1996:36-47.

38. Abbey SE. Psychiatric and diagnostic overlap in Chronic Fatigue Syndrome. In: Demitrack MA, Abbey SE, eds. Chronic Fatigue Syndrome–An Integrative Approach to Evaluation and Treatment. New York: The Guilford Press, 1996:48-71.

39. Hotopf M, Noah N, Wessely S. Chronic fatigue and minor psychiatric morbidity after viral meningitis: a controlled study. J Neurol Neurosurg Psychiatry 1996;60:504-509.

40. Wessely S, Chalder T, Hirsch S, Wallace P, Wright D. Psychological symptoms, somatic symptoms, and psychiatric disorder in chronic fatigue and chronic fatigue syndrome: a prospective study in the primary care setting. Am J Psychiatry 1996;153:1050-1059.

41. Petrie K, Moss-Morris R, Weinman J. The impact of catastrophic beliefs on functioning in chronic fatigue syndrome. J Psychosom Res 1995;39:31-37.

42. Ray C, Weir WR, Cullen S, Phillips S. Illness perception and symptom components in chronic fatigue syndrome. J Psychosom Res 1992;36:243-256.

43. Antoni MH, Bickman A, Lutgendorf S, Klimas N, et al. Psychosocial correlates of illness burden in chronic fatigue syndrome. Clin Infect Dis 1994;18:S73-S78.(abst)

44. Butler S, Chalder T, Ron M, Wessely S. Cognitive behavioral therapy in chronic fatigue syndrome. J Neurol Neurosurg Psychiatry 1991;54:153-158.(abst)

45. Wessely S. Cognitive Behavioral Therapy for patients with Chronic Fatigue Syndrome: Why. In: Demitrack MA, Abbey SE, eds. Chronic Fatigue Syndrome–An Integrative Approach to Evaluation and Treatment. New York: The Guilford Press, 1996:212-239.

46. Sharpe MC. Cognitive Behavioral Therapy for patients with Chronic Fatigue Syndrome: How. In: Demitrack MA, Abbey SE, eds. Chronic Fatigue Syndrome–An Integrative Approach to Evaluation and Treatment. New York: The Guilford Press, 1996:240

47. Lloyd AR, Hickie I, Brockman A, et al. Immunologic and psychologic therapy for patients with chronic fatigue syndrome: a double-blind, placebo-controlled trial [see comments]. Am J Med 1993;94:197-203.

48. Friedberg F, Krupp LB. A comparison of cognitive behavioral treatment for chronic fatigue syndrome and primary depression [see comments]. Clin Infect Dis 1994;18 Suppl 1:S105-10.

49. Abbey SE. Psychotherapeutic Perspectives in Chronic Fatigue Syndrome. In: Demitrack MA, Abbey SE, eds. Chronic Fatigue Syndrome–An Integrative Approach to Evaluation and Treatment. New York: The Guilford Press, 1996: 182-211.

50. Abbey SE. Somatization, illness attribution and the sociocultural psychiatry of chronic fatigue syndrome. Ciba Found Symp 1993;173:238-52; discussion 252-6.

51. Ware NC. Society, mind and body in chronic fatigue syndrome: an anthropological view. Ciba Found Symp 1993;173:62-73; discussion 73-82.

52. McKenzie R, Straus SE. Chronic fatigue syndrome. Adv Intern Med 1995;40:119-53.

53. Dale JK, Straus SE. The chronic fatigue syndrome: considerations relevant to children and adolescents. Adv Pediatr Infect Dis 1992;7:63-83.

54. Moldofsky H. Fibromyalgia, sleep disorder and chronic fatigue syndrome. Ciba Found Symp 1993;173:262-71; discussion 272-9.

55. Hotopf MH, Wessely S. Viruses, neurosis and fatigue [see comments]. J Psychosom Res 1994;38:499-514.

56. Goldenberg DL. Fibromyalgia, chronic fatigue syndrome, and myofascial pain. Curr Opin Rheumatol 1996;8:113-123.

57. Moldofsky H. Sleep, neuroimmune and neuroendocrine functions in fibromyalgia and chronic fatigue syndrome. Adv Neuroimmunol 1995;5:39-56.

58. Fiedler N, Kipen HM, Deluca J, Kelly-McNeil K, Natelson B. A controlled comparison of multiple chemical sensitivities and chronic fatigue syndrome. Psychosom Med 1996;58:38-49.

59. Ray C, Jefferies S, Weir WR. Life-events and the course of chronic fatigue syndrome. Br J Med Psychol 1995;68:323-331.

60. Krupp LB, Pollina D. Neuroimmune and neuropsychiatric aspects of chronic fatigue syndrome. Adv Neuroimmunol 1996;6:155-167.

61. Fukuda K, Straus SE, Hickie I, Sharpe MC, Dobbins JG, Komaroff A. The chronic fatigue syndrome: a comprehensive approach to its definition and study. International Chronic Fatigue Syndrome Study Group [see comments]. Ann Intern Med 1994;121:953-959.

62. Barrows DM. Functional capacity evaluations of persons with chronic fatigue immune dysfunction syndrome. Am J Occup Ther 1995;49:327-337.

63. Durack DT, Street AC. Fever of unknown origin–reexamined and redefined. Curr Clin Top Infect Dis 1991;11:35-51.

64. Holmes GP, Kaplan JE, Gantz NM, et al. Chronic fatigue syndrome: a working case definition. Ann Intern Med 1988;108:387-389.

65. Levine PH, Jacobson S, Pocinki AG, et al. Clinical, epidemiologic, and virologic studies in four clusters of the chronic fatigue syndrome [see comments]. Arch Intern Med 1992;152:1611-1616.

66. Peterson PK, Schenck C. Chronic fatigue syndrome as a "real" disease? [letter; comment]. J Gen Intern Med 1992;7:119-120.

67. Straus SE, Komaroff AL, Wedner HJ. Chronic fatigue syndrome: point and counterpoint. J Infect Dis 1994;170:1-6.

68. Farrar DJ, Locke SE, Kantrowitz FG. Chronic fatigue syndrome. 1: Etiology and pathogenesis. Behav Med 1995;21:5-16.

69. Briggs NC, Levine PH. A comparative review of systemic and neurological symptomatology in 12 outbreaks collectively described as chronic fatigue syndrome, epidemic neuromyasthenia, and myalgic encephalomyelitis. Clin Infect Dis 1994;18 Suppl 1:S32-42.

Impairment of Patients with Chronic Fatigue Syndrome

Barry Make, MD
James F. Jones, MD

INTRODUCTION

Individuals with chronic fatigue syndrome (CFS) commonly experience limitations in their ability to perform physical activities. This impaired functional capacity is associated with chronic and intermittent fatigue. In addition, patients note symptoms of increased fatigue, muscle weakness, and muscle pain which occur within the 48 hours following intensive activity such as strenuous exercise (1). These symptoms are of such paramount importance that they have been incorporated into the definition of this condition (2,3).

Patients with CFS are often so limited by their illness that they note an

Barry Make is Director, Pulmonary Rehabilitation, National Jewish Medical and Research Center, and Professor of Medicine, Division of Pulmonary Sciences and Critical Care Medicine, University of Colorado School of Medicine, Denver, CO, USA.

James F. Jones is Professor of Pediatrics, National Jewish Medical and Research Center, University of Colorado School of Medicine, Denver, CO.

Address correspondence to: Barry Make, MD, National Jewish Medical and Research Center, 1400 Jackson Street, B108, Denver, CO 80206.

Supported in part by NIH.

Presented in part at the 1996 AACFS Chronic Fatigue Conference, San Francisco, CA.

[Haworth co-indexing entry note]: "Impairment of Patients with Chronic Fatigue Syndrome." Make, Barry, and James F. Jones. Co-published simultaneously in *Journal of Chronic Fatigue Syndrome* (The Haworth Medical Press, an imprint of The Haworth Press, Inc.) Vol. 3, No. 4, 1997, pp. 43-55; and: *Disability and Chronic Fatigue Syndrome: Clinical, Legal and Patient Perspectives* (ed: Nancy G. Klimas, and Roberto Patarca) The Haworth Medical Press, an imprint of The Haworth Press, Inc., 1997, pp. 43-55. Single or multiple copies of this article are available for a fee from The Haworth Document Delivery Service [1-800-342-9678, 9:00 a.m. - 5:00 p.m. (EST). E-mail address: getinfo@haworth.com].

inability to perform even routine daily activities, and they are also unable to carry out job-related functions in the workplace. Physicians are called upon to assist in the determination of the physical and physiologic capacity of patients with CFS, but there is only scant published information on this subject (4,5,6). Moreover, there is little conceptual information to guide the physician in the process of determining physical impairment in CFS (7). As a result, Loveless et al. have noted that CFS patients have difficulty obtaining disability (8).

In order to develop a framework for determining physical impairment, this manuscript will: describe the results of investigations at National Jewish Medical and Research Center on muscle strength, endurance, fatigue and exercise capacity in chronic fatigue syndrome; use the American Medical Association guidelines for impairment rating of abnormalities of the respiratory system (9) to develop an impairment rating system for chronic fatigue syndrome; and apply the impairment rating system to CFS patients seen at National Jewish.

METHODS

As part of an multi-year NIH grant to explore the clinical features and mechanisms in chronic fatigue syndrome, we have prospectively investigated muscle function and exercise capacity, along with sleep, measures of diurnal pattern, autonomic function and inflammatory mediators in patients with CFS and in three groups of control subjects. For this report, we reviewed the results of muscle function and exercise capacity.

Study Subjects. Subjects with CFS were chosen from patients seen at National Jewish who met the 1988 definition of this disorder as proposed by Holmes et al. (2). All patients were ambulatory, were not experiencing an exacerbation and were able to complete a battery of other evaluations within three weeks following exercise and muscle tests. Muscle function and exercise in patients with CFS were compared with those obtained in three other groups of individuals: individuals with clinical depression, patients with allergic rhinitis, and healthy subjects of similar age and sex. Patients with CFS have been noted to be depressed, although this may be secondary to CFS and not a primary disorder. Thus, a group of patients with depression who were of similar age and sex to the CFS patients were recruited as one comparison group. It has been further suggested that CFS may be a disorder of chronic inflammation; thus patients with allergic rhinitis who were not taking oral corticosteroids were recruited as another comparison group. Finally, a group of healthy subjects of similar age and sex to the CFS patients was evaluated to serve as controls.

We studied 13 patients with CFS, 9 patients with depression, 12 patients with allergic rhinitis and 10 healthy controls. There were similar numbers of females and males in each group, and there were no statistical differences in the age (p = 0.06 by Fisher's protected least significant differences), weight (p = 0.7), and height (p = 0.5) of these 4 groups of subjects, depicted in Table 1.

Measurement of Muscle Strength. To evaluate whether muscle strength was reduced in patients with CFS as compared to control subjects, isokinetic muscle testing of the knee flexors and extensors and elbow flexors and extensors on the patient's dominant side was assessed. For this test, the patient was instructed to flex and extend the extremity as hard and as fast as possible in rapid succession without a rest 5 times against the resisting arm of an isokinetic muscle test machine (Cybex 6000, Cybex Division of Lumex, Rotowanda, NY). Peak torque, work and power of the flexors and extensors of the dominant extremity were recorded. The highest values from the five successive efforts were used for analysis. Results were expressed in absolute values and also as a percent of body weight.

Measurement of Muscle Fatigue and Recovery. Since patients complain of increased fatigue, decreased endurance and delayed recovery, these parameters were also assessed in the same muscle groups following measurement of muscle strength and using the same isokinetic muscle testing equipment. Fatigue was induced by having the patient perform repeated flexion and extension of the knee and elbow on the isokinetic muscle testing apparatus. Fatigue was defined as the number of flexion-extension

TABLE 1. Characteristics of Study Subjects

	CFS	ALLERGIC	DEPRESSION	CONTROLS	p*
NUMBER	13	12	9	10	
AGE (years)	38.8 ± 1.7	42.0 ± 2.8	43.1 ± 1.4	46.8 ± 1.4	0.06
SEX (Female/Male)	11/2	11/1	8/1	10/0	
WEIGHT (kg)	70.2 ± 5.5	73.2 ± 6.7	71.7 ± 4.0	64.2 ± 4.1	0.69
HEIGHT (cm)	167.2 ± 1.8	164.5 ± 2.5	168.2 ± 3.1	163.7 ± 1.8	0.49

Values are mean ± standard error.
* Analysis of variance

repetitions required to reduce peak torque by 50%. The number of repetitions required to reach the fatigue point was assessed on CFS patients and the three control groups.

Recovery was defined as the ability of muscles to recover from a fatiguing activity. To assess recovery, strength testing was repeated at five, ten and fifteen minutes following the development of fatigue using the Cybex equipment.

Exercise Capacity Measurement. To determine the effect of CFS on functional capacity, we performed a maximum incremental exercise test in patients with CFS and the three comparison groups identified above. Subjects were asked to report to the laboratory in the morning following only a light breakfast. An exercise test was performed on an electronically-braked bicycle ergometer with 1-minute increments in workload according to the method of Wasserman et al. (10). The initial workload and increments in workload were based upon each patient's predicted maximal exercise capacity and assessment of each patient's perceived limitation in physical activity, if present. For example, if the patient's predicted workload was 100 watts, based upon subjective assessment, the patient was believed to have only 50% of predicted (i.e., 50 watts) exercise capacity, then the initial workload was unloaded pedaling and 5 watt test increments were employed. The increments were chosen to obtain a total exercise duration of approximately 8-10 minutes which is believed to be optimal test duration (10); a longer duration of testing is generally believed to be more representative of an endurance rather than a maximal test. Patients were encouraged to exercise until they could no longer continue because of symptoms of dyspnea or leg discomfort. Continuous EKG monitoring was performed during exercise to assess heart rate; none of the patients developed evidence of cardiac ischemia during exercise. All subjects breathed room air through a mouthpiece, and measurements of expired gas were performed to assess fraction of expired oxygen for measurement of oxygen consumption using a SensorMedics 2900 Energy Expenditure Unit (SensorMedics, Yorba Linda, CA). Maximal workload was recorded as the maximal work which the patient could achieve for at least 30 seconds on the cycle ergometer.

RESULTS

Muscle Function in CFS. The results showed no statistical differences in peak torque, work, and power of the flexors and extensors of the knees and elbows in patients with CFS as compared to control subjects. Table 2 provides information only on peak torque of the knees; for the sake of brevity, data on work and power of the knees and results of elbow flexors and extensors are not shown due to the large number of indices measured. Correcting strength measurements for body weight did not alter the results of the analysis.

Table 2 provides the results of muscle fatigue testing. Based on these results, patients with CFS do not have increased fatigability of the knee and elbow extensors and flexors compared to control subjects. The results after 10 minutes of recovery are shown in Table 2 and are not different in each of the groups. Similarly at each of the other recovery time points (i.e., 5 and 15 minutes), patients with CFS recovered muscle strength in manner similar to the three comparison groups.

Based on these studies, strength of the knee and elbow flexors and extensions appears to be normal in CFS when compared to healthy controls, patients with depression, and individuals with allergic rhinitis. In addition, endurance and recovery following fatigue are also normal in CFS patients.

Exercise Capacity. The primary measures of exercise capacity were the maximum amount of work and maximal oxygen consumption achieved during the test. To correct for age and sex, the results of these parameters are expressed in Table 3 as percent predicted using the normal values of Wasserman et al. (10).

The results of exercise testing indicate that patients with CFS have reduced maximal work and oxygen consumption (p = 0.001 and 0.01 respectively by analysis of variance) compared to the three other comparison groups of subjects studied. There were no statistical differences in

TABLE 2. Muscle Function of the Knee Flexors in CFS and Comparison Subjects

	CFS	ALLERGIC	DEPRESSION	CONTROLS	p*
STRENGTH (Peak Torque, ft - lbs)	36.8 ± 4.1	42.9 ± 4.3	53.2 ± 5.0	45.5 ± 5.0	0.1
FATIGUE (Repetitions to fatigue, #)	18.7 ± 9.6	25.4 ± 2.1	22.8 ± 2.7	24.7 ± 1.4	0.2
RECOVERY (Peak Torque 10 minutes after fatigue. ft - lbs)	39.5 ± 4.0	47.3 ± 4.1	54.2 ± 4.8	47.1 ± 4.8	0.14

* Analysis of variance

TABLE 3. Exercise Capacity in CFS and Comparison Subjects

	CFS	ALLERGIC	DEPRESSION	CONTROLS	p*
WORK max (% predicted)	76.3 ± 6.2	107.3 ± 7.8	91.7 ± 4.9	109.9 ± 3.7	0.001**
OXYGEN CONSUMPTION max (% predicted)	62.9 ± 4.8	92.8 ± 6.3	82.7 ± 4.5	87.3 ± 3.0	0.01***
HEART RATE max (% predicted)	83.9 ± 3.4	84.9 ± 2.3	89.1 ± 3.4	92.2 ± 2.4	0.19

* Analysis of variance
** Using Fisher's protected least significant differences at the 0.05 level, CFS patients had lower values than control and allergy subjects.
*** Using Fisher's protected least significant differences at the 0.05 level, CFS patients had lower values than control and allergy subjects.

these parameters between the three comparison groups (allergic rhinitis, depression, healthy controls). The cause of the reduced exercise capacity is unclear. Patients with CFS achieved a similar maximal heart rate compared to the other three groups of comparison subjects and all achieved a respiratory quotient of $\geq$ 1.0. Thus, it appeared that patients exercised to their maximal capacity and did not terminate the exercise voluntarily. There was no clinical indication of cardiac disease and no evidence of ischemia or arrhythmia on EKG during the exercise in any of the subjects.

DISCUSSION

This results of the current study indicate that patients with CFS have normal muscle strength of the knees and elbows measured by isokinetic testing. Muscle strength has also been reported to be normal in CFS and similar to controls in other studies (11,12). One study evaluating muscle function in response to exercise found comparable isometric voluntary contraction and relaxation rates in CFS and controls after symptom-limited incremental cycle exercise (12). However, muscle function was also normal before exercise in these subjects. Isometric testing used during most of the previous studies of patients with CFS does not mimic muscle function required for most daily activities and thus may not be expected to correlate with symptoms occurring during normal activity. In our study, the use of isokinetic testing was employed as a more functional method of assessing muscle strength.

Our results indicate that muscles fatigue normally and recover in a manner similar to control subjects. Given the prominence of patient symptoms of fatigue, other investigators have also evaluated muscle fatigue (11,13). A previous study found delayed recovery of peak torque following isometrically induced fatigue of the elbow (14). In another study which evaluated isometric exercise of the tibialis anterior muscle in normals and patients with CFS, voluntary stimulation during maximal sustained exercise was found to be reduced in patients with CFS (13). This study suggests that the failure of CFS patients to maximally activate skeletal muscles which have normal intrinsic functional capacity may be related to a central rather than peripheral component of muscle fatigue. However, in another study patients were voluntarily able to maximally activate their elbow muscles during an isometric contraction, and additional electrical stimulation (twitch occlusion) did not produce additional muscle contraction (11). Thus, previous studies provide conflicting results concerning muscle fatigue in CFS.

The results of this study demonstrate that patients with CFS have reduced maximal exercise capacity on a bicycle ergometer. Similar results have been noted by Riley et al., who demonstrated a reduced exercise capacity in patients with CFS compared to healthy controls and patients with irritable bowel syndrome (6). These investigators employed symptom-limited maximal exercise capacity on a treadmill using a Bruce protocol. Patients with CFS also had higher heart rate and higher blood lactate concentrations at submaximal levels of exertion. Despite the reduced exercise capacity, subjects with CFS had a higher level of perceived exertion. The high lactate, heart rate and perceived exertion are indicators that CFS patients likely achieved their maximal exercise capacity. However, reduced exercise capacity has not been universally found in CFS. For example, Edwards et al. have shown similar incremental bicycle ergometry exercise in CFS and controls (15).

Impairment and Disability

Impairment is defined as an alteration in health status which is assessed by medical methods. Integral to the concept of impairment are the medical diagnosis and medical considerations of disease or disorder in an organ, system or even in the entire body. For purposes of this discussion, it is assumed that the clinician has established a clinical diagnosis of CFS and excluded other conditions with the use of appropriate laboratory tests. Impairment also incorporates the ability of the organ, system or body to perform its normal functions. In CFS patients, the ability to perform physical activity should therefore be assessed as a guide to determination of impairment.

When the physician has established a rating of impairment, this information may then be used to make a determination of disability. Disability refers to a person's capacity to meet personal, social or occupational demands. More simply, disability is the gap between what an individual can do and what he/she desires or needs to do. However, disability is not a medical assessment but rather may be more appropriately considered as a social, societal, legislative, or regulatory determination. In practice, the Social Security Administration has developed regulations to guide the determination of disability (8).

AMA Guidelines for Impairment Rating. The American Medical Association (AMA) has published guidelines for rating of impairment which are almost universally used to assess impairment and which incorporate the results of objective diagnostic testing (9). In patients with respiratory disorders, the AMA guidelines suggest the use of such tests as spirometry and diffusing capacity. Based upon the symptoms in patients with CFS, pulmonary physiologic testing of the function of the lungs is likely to be less important as a guide to impairment in CFS than in primary disorders of the lungs. Indeed, our evaluations have indicated that spirometry is normal in patients with CFS. However, the AMA guidelines also provide suggestions for impairment based upon exercise testing, which we and others have shown is likely to be abnormal in patients with CFS who note difficulty performing physical activity. Since impairment ratings, according to Social Security Administration policy (8), should not be based upon symptoms alone, exercise testing might be an appropriate basis for impairment rating. The classes of impairment, degree of impairment, and oxygen consumption ranges from the AMA impairment guidelines are summarized in Table 4.

Physical capacity based upon exercise tolerance is only one of a number of factors which might be considered in a more global impairment rating. It might also be possible to incorporate objective measures of muscle strength, endurance and recovery into an impairment rating. However, there are no established guidelines that are based upon the unique set of symptoms noted by CFS patients. In addition, our results indicate that CFS patients have normal muscle strength, endurance and recovery, and there are no uniformly observed abnormalities in other reports. Thus, objective testing cannot be recommended to classify degree of muscle impairment in CFS. Nevertheless, if objective abnormalities in muscle function are documented using other tests, then guidelines for impairment

TABLE 4. Classes of Impairment*

	CLASS 1	CLASS 2	CLASS 3	CLASS 4
DEGREE OF IMPAIRMENT	0%	10-25%	30-45%	50-100%
DESCRIPTION	No impairment of the whole person	Mild impairment of the whole person	Moderate impairment of the whole person	Severe impairment of the whole person
MAXIMAL OXYGEN CONSUMPTION	> 25 ml/min/kg	20-25 ml/min/kg	15-20 ml/min/kg	< 15 ml/min/kg

* Based upon AMA Guidelines for Impairment Rating (8)

ratings using these indices could be developed in the future. Similarly, other measures, such as indices of cognitive function, might be incorporated into an impairment rating. However, the purpose of this study was limited to measures of physical capacity. The AMA guidelines indicate that impairment be rated after maximum medical improvement. The waxing and waning of the illness in patients with CFS raises the question of how to best assign impairment ratings in an illness marked by frequent exacerbations.

Impairment in Patients with CFS. We had the opportunity to perform exercise tests on an additional six subjects who also fulfilled the definition of CFS (2,3). The 13 CFS patients presented above and the additional 6 patients were thus available to be classified by their degree of impairment. As shown in Figure 1, the majority of our patients (16 of 19) with CFS have some degree of impairment: only 3 patients have no impairment–impairment Class I; 3 patients are mildly impaired (20-25 ml O_2/min/kg maximal oxygen consumption)–impairment Class II; 8 patients are moderately impaired (VO_2 max 15-20 ml O_2/min/kg)–impairment Class III; and 5 patients are severely impaired (<15 ml O_2/min/kg)–impairment Class IV.

An alternate method of assessing the physical capacity of patients by physical and occupational therapists during rehabilitation is to assess their ability to perform activity based upon the exercise level achieved. This is often expressed as metabolic equivalents (mets). One met is equal to the resting oxygen consumption–the amount of energy required at rest. One met may also be considered to be equivalent to 3.5 ml of oxygen consumption/min/kg of body weight, the usual energy expenditure at rest. Expression of maximal exercise capacity as the maximum met level achieved during a formal exercise test can be used to define the functional activity which may be expected in a given individual. The amount of work re-

FIGURE 1. Number of patients with CFS in each of the four degrees of impairment based upon maximal oxygen consumption. Classes of impairment based upon Table 4.

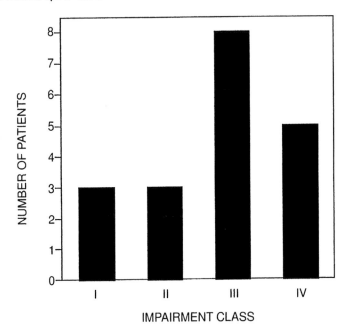

quired during daily and vocational activities can be expressed as the number of mets required for the activity. By definition, sitting at rest is equivalent to one met. Dressing uses about 2.3 mets; driving a car, 2.8 mets; washing clothes, 3.0 mets, walking, 2.5 miles/hour, 3.6 mets; golfing, 5.0 mets; gardening, 5.8 mets; and carpentry, 6.8 mets. It should be emphasized that patients can maintain their maximal level of activity (maximal met level) for only a very brief time. Thus, although a patient with a measured maximal exercise capacity of 3.6 mets may be able to walk at 2.5 miles per hour, the patient can sustain this activity for only a limited amount of time.

The met levels (based upon 1 met = 3.5 ml of oxygen consumption/min/kg of body weight) achieved by the 19 CFS patients compared to patients with allergic rhinitis, depression and healthy controls are depicted in Figure 2. It is clear that although there is a wide range in the maximum met levels achieved by patients with CFS, many CFS patients are unable to perform many of the activities required during the course of their daily lives. By contrast, all subjects in the other groups can be expected to

FIGURE 2. Met levels achieved during maximal cycle ergometry in 19 patients with CFS compared to patients with allergic rhinitis (A), depression (D), and healthy controls (C). Means and standard errors for each group are depicted.

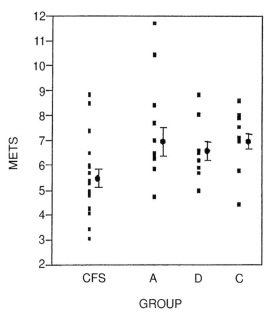

perform activities of daily living and only one patient in each of the four comparison groups has met levels below 5.5.

CONCLUSION

This study of patients with CFS documents normal muscle strength, endurance and recovery from fatigue. However, maximal exercise capacity measured on a cycle ergometer is reduced to 76% of predicted workload, a significant decrease compared to patients of similar age and sex who have depression, patients with allergic rhinitis, and healthy controls.

Using published guidelines for rating of impairment, a system to classify the impairment of patients with CFS is proposed which is consistent with existing guidelines used for other diseases. Since measured muscle function is normal in CFS, indices of function of individual muscle groups are not included in the impairment rating. The classification scheme is objective and based solely upon measured maximal exercise capacity. The results of maximal bicycle ergometry in a group of 19 CFS patients suggest that many patients with CFS are impaired. Further validation of this impairment rating is suggested before it can be recommended for widespread use in CFS. Additional attempts to objectively quantify the other symptoms in patients with CFS may also be useful in the determination of impairment ratings.

ACKNOWLEDGMENTS

The authors wish to express their appreciation to staff of the Rehabilitation Services Department for assistance in assessing muscle function, the staff of the Pulmonary Physiology Unit for assistance in assessing exercise capacity, and to Ms. Tilli Urban and Mary Ellen Klein for their excellent secretarial assistance.

REFERENCES

1. Wessely S, Powell R. Fatigue syndrome: a comparison of chronic "postviral" fatigue with neuromuscular and affective disorders. *J Neurol Neurosurg Psych* 1989; 52:940-948.

2. Holmes G, Kaplan J, Gantz N, Komaroff A, Schoneberger L, Straus S, Jones J, Dubois R, Cunningham-Rundles C, Pahwa S, Tosato G, Zegans L, Purtilo D, Brown N, Schooley R, Brus I. Chronic fatigue syndrome: a working case definition. *Ann Intern Med* 1988; 108:387-389.

3. Fukuda K, Straus SE, Hickie I, Sharpe MC, Dobbins JG, Komaroff A, Group C. Chronic fatigue syndrome: A comprehensive approach to its definition and study. *Ann Intern Med* 1994; 121:953-9.

4. Stevens S. Using exercise testing to document functional disability in CFS. *JCFS* 1995; 1:127-129.

5. Sisto SA, LaManca J, Cordero DL, et al. Metabolic and cardiovascular effects of a progressive exercise test in patients with chronic fatigue syndrome. *Am J Med* 1996; 100:634-40.

6. Riley MS, O'Brien CJ, McCluskey DR, Bell NP, Nicholls DP. Aerobic work capacity in patients with chronic fatigue syndrome. *Br Med J* 1990; 301: 953-956.

7. Loveless MO, Lloyd A, Perpich R. Summary of public policy and chronic fatigue syndrome: a perspective. *Clin Inf Dis* 1994; 18 (Suppl 1):S163-55.

8. Providing medical evidence to the Social Security Administration for individuals with chronic fatigue syndrome: A guide for health professionals. 64-063.

9. *Guide to the evaluation of permanent impairment.* 3rd. ed. Chicago: American Medical Association, 1990.

10. Wasserman K, Hansen JE, Sue DY, Whipp BJ. *Principles of Exercise Testing and Interpretation.* Philadelphia: Lea and Febiger, 1987.

11. Lloyd AR, Gandevia SC, Hales JP. Muscle performance, voluntary activation, twitch properties and perceived effort in normal subjects and patients with the chronic fatigue syndrome. *Brain* 1991; 114:85-98.

12. Gibson H, Carroll N, Clague J, Edwards R. Exercise performance and fatiguability in patients with chronic fatigue syndrome. *J Neurol Neurosurg Psych* 1993; 56:993-998.

13. Kent-Braun JA, Sharma KR, Weiner MW, Massie B, Miller RG. Central basis of muscle fatigue in chronic fatigue syndrome. *Neurology* 1993; 43:125-131.

14. Lloyd AR, Phales J, Gandevia SC. Muscle strength, endurance and recovery in the post-infection fatigue syndrome. *J Neurol Neurosurg Psych* 1988; 51:1316-1322.

15. Edwards R, Gibson H, Clague J, Helliwell T. Muscle histopathology and physiology in chronic fatigue syndrome. *Ciba Foundation Symposium* 1993; 173:102-117.

THE LEGAL PERSPECTIVE

Social Security Disability Program

Thomas L. Gloss

For the person with chronic fatigue syndrome (CFS), the ability to work is often compromised, resulting in the person's applying for one or more kinds of disability benefits. Usually, after exhausting all of the available short-term benefits, the person turns to Social Security. Social Security's relatively strict definition of disability and the sometimes lengthy determination process can raise questions for both the person and his or her health care provider. The following information should provide the health care provider with a better understanding of Social Security's programs, requirements and disability determination process.

The Social Security Administration (SSA) administers two disability programs, Social Security Disability Insurance (SSDI) and Supplemental Security Income (SSI). SSDI, a social insurance program funded through contributions paid by workers and their employers, covers disabled workers, their dependents, their widows(ers) and their disabled adult children.

Thomas L. Gloss is Special Assistant to Associate Commissioner for Disability, Office of Disability, Social Security Administration, Room 545 Altmeyer Building, 6401 Security Boulevard, Baltimore, MD 21235.

[Haworth co-indexing entry note]: "Social Security Disability Program." Gloss, Thomas L. Co-published simultaneously in *Journal of Chronic Fatigue Syndrome* (The Haworth Medical Press, an imprint of The Haworth Press, Inc.) Vol. 3, No. 4, 1997, pp. 57-61; and: *Disability and Chronic Fatigue Syndrome: Clinical, Legal and Patient Perspectives* (ed: Nancy G. Klimas, and Roberto Patarca) The Haworth Medical Press, an imprint of The Haworth Press, Inc., 1997, pp. 57-61. Single or multiple copies of this article are available for a fee from The Haworth Document Delivery Service [1-800-342-9678, 9:00 a.m. - 5:00 p.m. (EST). E-mail address: getinfo@haworth.com].

Eligibility for SSDI benefits is based on an individual's work history, and the amount of the benefit is based on the individual's earnings. SSDI requires a 5-month waiting period for cash benefits and provides Medicare coverage after 24 months of disability. SSI, however, is paid to disabled or blind adults and children on the basis of limited income and resources, and the monthly Federal payment is a fixed amount, although some States supplement the Federal payment. Also, in most States, Medicaid benefits are linked to SSI entitlement. There is no mandatory waiting period for SSI or Medicaid.

During 1996, SSA paid about $70 billion in SSDI and SSI benefits to more than 8 million people with disabilities. SSA receives about 3 million new applications for disability benefits each year; about half of those ultimately are approved for benefits. Of the applications approved during the past year, approximately 75 per cent were allowed at the first two steps of the administrative process (the initial and reconsideration levels).

The definition of disability is the same for both programs; i.e., to be considered disabled under the Social Security Act, an individual must be unable "to engage in any substantial gainful activity by reason of any medically-determinable physical or mental impairment which can be expected to result in death or has lasted or can be expected to last for a continuous period of not less than 12 months."

The disability determination for each claimant at both the initial and reconsideration levels is made by an agency in each State, called the Disability Determination Services (DDS). The DDSs are fully funded by the Federal government and are responsible for developing medical evidence to determine whether a claimant is disabled under the law and for determining when disability began and/or ended. The DDSs use a team approach, combining a physician or psychologist with a disability examiner, in reviewing the medical evidence and making the disability determination.

The DDS requests medical evidence of record–specifically, information about the claimant's impairment(s)–from the treating sources (those physicians, psychologists, hospitals, clinics, etc., identified by the claimant on the disability application). This evidence is the most important evidence in the process because it provides a longitudinal picture of the claimant's impairment(s). However, if this evidence is insufficient to make a determination, the DDS will purchase a consultative examination from the treating source or from an independent source.

The individual's impairment must result from anatomical, physiological or psychological abnormalities which can be shown by medically acceptable clinical and laboratory diagnostic techniques. A physical or mental impairment must be established by medical evidence consisting of signs, symptoms and laboratory findings. The impairment may not be established on the basis of symptoms alone, but symptoms are considered in evaluating the impairment.

In adult disability cases, a 5-step sequential evaluation process is used to determine if the individual is disabled. This process first considers if the individual is working. If the person is not working, or has earnings considered not "substantial," the DDS reviews the medical evidence to decide whether the impairment is severe or not severe. To be severe, the impairment must have more than a minimal impact on the individual's ability to perform basic work activities. Once a severe impairment is found, then the severity of that impairment is compared to the severity of those contained in SSA's Listing of Impairments. Where the level of severity meets or equals that which is listed, the individual is found disabled and the adjudication process stops.

For individuals whose impairment does not meet or equal the listed severity, the DDS determines the person's residual functional capacity for work activity. This is compared with the functional requirements of the person's past work and other work available in the national economy. The person's age and education are also considered in deciding if there is any other work he or she can do. The individual is found to be disabled if unable to do his or her past relevant work or any other work existing in the national economy.

In all cases, including CFS, symptoms alone will not result in an allowance of disability. As stated above, there must be a medically determinable physiological or psychological impairment based on objective signs, symptoms and laboratory findings. There is no medical listing specifically for CFS, but individuals may have a documented impairment, or combination of impairments, that is so severe that it does meet or equal the severity of one or more listed impairments.

SSA has been reviewing disability claims involving CFS since 1985, at which time it was commonly called Chronic Epstein-Barr Virus Syndrome. Early on, CFS proved to be a challenging disorder for SSA to evaluate due to the lack of uniformly agreed upon medically acceptable clinical signs or laboratory findings which are required for SSA to establish the existence of a medically determinable impairment under the law. In 1993, however, SSA issued detailed policy guidance to all of its adjudicators explaining what types of evidence must be pursued in order to properly evaluate CFS.

In accordance with that guidance, claims for disability on the basis of CFS are currently documented and evaluated on an individual case-by-case basis considering the totality of the evidence and the disease process as it impacts the individual's functional capabilities. A well-documented disability case record over a period of 12 or more months reflecting ongoing medical assessment and treatment with periodic evaluations of the claimant's response to such treatment provides the most useful information upon which to base decisions concerning the presence of a medically determinable impairment in cases involving CFS. Certain clinical findings are frequently seen in longitudinal clinical records and may provide substantiation of a medically determinable impairment when viewed in the context of a well-documented medical record. These findings include such signs as recurrent, documented fever, clinically documented lymphadenopathy, clinically documented pharyngitis, neurally mediated hypotension as documented by tilt table testing, and/or clinically confirmed depression or other mental impairment. When seen in association with fatigue and the constellation of other related symptoms surrounding CFS, these types of clinical findings can substantiate the presence of a medically determinable impairment.

Under this adjudicative approach, once a medically determinable impairment has been established which could reasonably be expected to cause symptoms such as fatigue, pain, etc., then those symptoms and their limiting effects upon the claimant must be considered both in determining the severity of the impairment and in assessing the residual functional capacity for the individual.

Treating health care providers can help in this process by providing complete longitudinal evidence that thoroughly describes the clinical condition(s) and treatment rendered. It is also helpful to indicate responses to treatment, adverse side effects of medications and/or other factors that contribute to the impairment. In February 1996, SSA published a CFS factsheet for health care providers to help publicize our medical documentation requirements. Copies of that factsheet are available by calling SSA's Public Information Distribution Center at (410) 965-0945 or on the Internet (at http://www.ssa.gov/odhome).

Since CFS can affect so many body systems, a person may have a condition that meets or equals the severity of a number of different listed impairments. Out of expediency for the applicant and SSA, the DDS ends medical development when it establishes a basis for finding the person disabled. In other words, SSA develops the case only to the point of allowing benefits. Therefore, if the adjudicator has enough evidence to find the person to be disabled based on any physical or mental impairment, he or she will not pursue what could be lengthy and expensive development to establish a second impairment (e.g., CFS) as the cause of the disability. This may be confusing to the person or the treating physician.

This situation also has an impact on people when SSA reviews their claims to determine if they are still disabled, commonly called a continuing disability review (CDR). When a person is found disabled by the DDS, a diary code is set for a CDR for about 1 year, 3 years or 7 years in the future, depending on whether medical improvement is expected, is possible, or is not expected. If a person with CFS was actually approved for disability based on meeting a mental impairment listing, the focus of the CDR will be improvement in the person's mental condition. The person probably assumed the basis for receiving disability was CFS, and may be shocked and/or upset to be asked questions at the CDR that focus on his or her mental status. It is important, however, that the person cooperate during the CDR and provide as much information as possible about all of his or her impairments. It is also important for health care providers to document all of the patient's complaints, symptoms and clinical findings at each visit, so the clinical record accurately reflects the person's condition over a longitudinal period.

SSA is continuing to perform special case reviews in order to help identify changes and improvements needed to our policy guidelines dealing with CFS. We are also working closely with The CFIDS Association of America, Inc., to identify and resolve adjudicative problems with claims involving CFS.

Disability Policy and CFIDS:
A Washington Perspective

Thomas F. Sheridan

SUMMARY. "Disability Policy and CFIDS: A Washington Perspective" provides a follow-up to Mr. Sheridan's remarks at the American Association for Chronic Fatigue Syndrome's clinical conference in San Francisco on October 16, 1996. In this article, Mr. Sheridan explains that the difficulty for people with CFIDS (PWCs) in obtaining disability benefits stems from the fact that disability determination is based on a person's functional impairments resulting from a particular diagnosis. In other words, the Social Security Administration does not consider a CFIDS diagnosis alone sufficient criteria to win a disability claim. The article also describes the advocacy efforts carried out over the past five years by The CFIDS Association of America and The Sheridan Group and the achievements of that collaboration. Mr. Sheridan concludes his article with advice for PWCs who are considering an application for SSA disability benefits. *[Article copies available for a fee from The Haworth Document Delivery Service: 1-800-342-9678. E-mail address: getinfo@ haworth.com]*

On October 16, 1997, I had the pleasure of participating in a panel discussion on disability at the American Association for Chronic Fatigue Syndrome's clinical conference in San Francisco. I had been invited to

Thomas F. Sheridan is associated with The Sheridan Group, Ltd., 1808 Swann Street, NW, Washington, DC 20009.

[Haworth co-indexing entry note]: "Disability Policy and CFIDS: A Washington Perspective." Sheridan, Thomas F. Co-published simultaneously in *Journal of Chronic Fatigue Syndrome* (The Haworth Medical Press, an imprint of The Haworth Press, Inc.) Vol. 3, No. 4, 1997, pp. 63-67; and: *Disability and Chronic Fatigue Syndrome: Clinical, Legal and Patient Perspectives* (ed: Nancy G. Klimas, and Roberto Patarca) The Haworth Medical Press, an imprint of The Haworth Press, Inc., 1997, pp. 63-67. Single or multiple copies of this article are available for a fee from The Haworth Document Delivery Service [1-800-342-9678, 9:00 a.m. - 5:00 p.m. (EST). E-mail address: getinfo@haworth.com].

63

speak on "The United States Congress and Disability Policy"–a rather extensive and complex issue. As the lobbyist for The CFIDS Association of America, I was happy to share a Washington perspective on disability policy vis-a-vis CFIDS and I welcome this opportunity to elaborate on my comments from that day.

The essential point of my remarks at the AACFS conference which I wish to reiterate in this article is that the difficulty for people with CFIDS (PWCs) in obtaining disability benefits stems from the fact that disability determination is not diagnosis driven, but is rather based on a person's functional impairments resulting from a particular diagnosis. In other words, in the eyes of the Social Security Administration and private long-term disability insurers, a CFIDS diagnosis alone is not enough to win a disability claim. The criteria for awarding disability benefits are whether a person is able to maintain substantial gainful activity (i.e., employment).

There are some dangers in attempting to summarize in simple terms such a complex subject, so I proceed with the disclaimer that while I shall try to provide some understanding of how that premise affects the ability of a person with CFIDS to obtain disability benefits, I do so not as an expert in disability policy but as an advocate who is providing an overview and, hopefully, some helpful advice for people who find themselves involved in the disability application process.

The Sheridan Group has represented The CFIDS Association of America since 1992. When we began to work together, our focus was on the need for expanded research on CFIDS and improved accountability by the federal government for federal dollars that were to be spent on CFIDS. The lack of research had negative consequences for the CFIDS community because without serious scientific inquiry there could be no real challenge to the characterization of chronic fatigue syndrome as "yuppie flu," a condition not to be taken seriously, or at best, to be treated as a mental illness.

Over the past five years, advocacy efforts on behalf of CFIDS have yielded substantial results, namely a 400% increase in the amount of federal funding that goes to the National Institutes of Health (NIH) and the Centers for Disease Control and Prevention (CDC) for CFIDS research. Indeed, during Congressional hearings for Fiscal Year 1997 appropriations, Congressman John Porter, Chairman of the Appropriations Subcommittee on Labor, Health and Human Services, and Education (the committee which provides funding for both NIH and CDC), made a point of highlighting the increased funding for chronic fatigue syndrome from zero to the $12 million in Fiscal Year 1996 and thanking The CFIDS Association of America for its part in bringing about that increase.

Accountability has been strengthened as well, with the establishment of the Department of Health and Human Services' CFS Interagency Coordinating Committee, where representatives of the federal agencies that are involved in CFIDS come together four times a year with CFIDS advocates to discuss their work on CFIDS. The existence of this committee raises the profile of CFIDS considerably and ensures a higher level of accountability than existed before its creation.

While the research is being conducted, people with CFIDS still have the day-to-day issues of living with a debilitating illness. For those people who become too ill to work, Social Security Disability Insurance (SSDI) or long-term disability insurance through one's employer is a life line. In too many cases, however, that life line is yanked out of reach when an application for disability benefits is denied. Again, the critical point is that under current rules, a person with CFIDS will not qualify on the basis of the diagnosis alone. For people with CFIDS, the disease manifests at varying degrees of disability and varying levels of severity over time. Some people experience the disease at relatively functional levels over long periods of time while others may experience completely disabling symptoms that last days, weeks, months, or years.

Unfortunately, the Social Security system is not designed to respond to these types of episodic instances of disability. Over the last few years, however, a number of disability and disease groups have slowly begun to challenge the system's ability to deal with short-term episodic illness or disabilities that may in fact vary in degrees of impairment over time. For example, testing positive for the Human Immunodeficiency Virus (HIV) denotes the presence of a virus but in itself is not necessarily a disabling condition. An AIDS diagnosis was generally assumed to be permanently disabling as well as fatal; however, with the advent of more effective treatments, some AIDS patients are rallying back from complete impairment to relative health. Conversely, some people with HIV infections can experience disabling opportunistic symptoms.

Another aspect to the debate over disability policy is the challenge issued by the disability rights movement questioning the assumption that people with "traditional disabilities" are incapable of work. They argue that many Americans with disabilities are employed and supporting themselves.

While these issues and concerns are being debated and sorted through, it is important for a person with CFIDS to have an understanding of the system as it currently exists in order to increase one's chances of successfully navigating the disability application process. First of all, Social Security Disability Insurance is available only to those Americans who have been employed and paid Social Security taxes over a defined period of time *and who have been determined to be disabled (functionally impaired) for the past twelve months.* This means that if your disability has not been documented for at least twelve months you may find yourself waiting for a period of time before benefits can begin. There are a few conditions that will automatically be assumed to be the onset of disability but CFIDS is not currently in that category.

The Social Security system is not designed to extend benefits automatically to those who apply. Indeed, the system is designed to screen out those whose disabilities are either insufficient to meet the standards of functional disability or whose claims are not valid or in compliance with existing criteria. In other words, when one approaches the disability determination process, one must be prepared to prove functional impairment. You are *not* "disabled 'til proven otherwise."

Access to SSDI is not only important for offsetting income lost by lack of employment but is also a vital link for many Americans to the Medicare system, which provides coverage for medical services to the disabled as well as to the elderly. Those who have not held employment and therefore cannot qualify for SSDI can seek assistance from Supplemental Security Insurance (SSI) and the Medicaid system. In order to qualify for Medicaid, one must be poor as well as disabled. A disability alone will not be sufficient to qualify for this program. Income and assets, while specifically defined by law, must be virtually non-existent before Medicaid benefits can be granted.

Despite the bleak picture that this brief overview paints, this is a period of great change. CFIDS is a relatively new disease with more unknown about it than known. There have been many battles and a few victories that have begun to move the disease closer to receiving adequate attention, response and research. The diagnostic criteria established by CDC with input from advocates in 1995 have helped establish a better baseline for determining those with CFIDS. The Social Security Administration has begun to track those cases reported to it by a CFIDS diagnostic code. This process, though only providing data, is helping us identify clogs in the system. The CFIDS Association of America has put a high priority on working with SSA and will continue to educate, at all levels, the personnel who make disability determinations for people with this illness. In stating its public policy goals for the next two years, The CFIDS Association of America has set the following strategies to effect positive change concerning SSA and PWCs:

- Participate in a series of roundtable meetings about barriers to Social Security Disability Income benefits proposed by the SSA's Office of Disability.

- Advocate for the inclusion of up-to-date, medically accurate information on CFIDS in the SSA's Listing of Impairments and POMS manuals.
- Monitor SSA-wide changes to determine impact on CFIDS patients and take appropriate actions to ensure greater responsiveness under new guidelines.
- Develop strategies to effectively address difficulties anticipated for CFIDS beneficiaries during Continuing Disability Reviews.

In closing, I would offer a few basic rules to follow when contemplating an application for SSA disability benefits:

- Have an established and respectful relationship with your physician;
- Tell your physician that you are considering an application and ask for his/her assistance;
- Remember that CFIDS in and of itself is not an impairment; use the CFIDS tracking code (688) if you are applying because of CFIDS-related impairments;
- Consult an attorney who specializes in disability claims. Most CFIDS applicants must appeal at least twice before approval;
- Start the process with the expectation that the process will be hard and long; prepare yourself emotionally, physically, and financially;
- Keep good records of all your medical interactions and your encounters with the Social Security system. If trouble looms, this information may be vital to your success.

Our goal must ultimately remain focused on finding the etiology of the disease because from there we may be able to then clearly distinguish the disease, its course, its level of progress and likely level of disability. There are things we can all do to make the system work better now, but the best results will come when medical research delivers the truth about this emerging health crisis.

A Primer
for Chronic Fatigue Syndrome Claimants
in Applying for Long-Term Disability
Policy Benefits

Stuart H. Sandhaus

THE LONG-TERM DISABILITY POLICY

For the purposes of this article, a long-term disability policy ("LTD policy") is a contract between an insurer and insured that provides income replacement for the insured, should that person become disabled from illness or injury and be unable to work. These contracts usually define disability as being either unable to continually perform the material duties of the insured's *own* occupation *or* unable to continually engage in the material duties of *any* occupation. Some LTD policies incorporate both of these definitions: for the first twenty-four months the insured need only be disabled from his/her *own* occupation and after this twenty-four month period the insured need only be disabled from *any* occupation.

COMMON POLICY LIMITATIONS

The ability of a person suffering from chronic fatigue syndrome (CFS) to continue to perform the material duties of any occupation is at issue

Stuart H. Sandhaus is Attorney at Law, Crown Cabot Financial Center, 28202 Cabot Road, Suite 300, Laguna Niguel, CA 92677.

[Haworth co-indexing entry note]: "A Primer for Chronic Fatigue Syndrome Claimants in Applying for Long-Term Disability Policy Benefits." Sandhaus, Stuart H. Co-published simultaneously in *Journal of Chronic Fatigue Syndrome* (The Haworth Medical Press, an imprint of The Haworth Press, Inc.) Vol. 3, No. 4, 1997, pp. 69-73; and: *Disability and Chronic Fatigue Syndrome: Clinical, Legal and Patient Perspectives* (ed: Nancy G. Klimas, and Roberto Patarca) The Haworth Medical Press, an imprint of The Haworth Press, Inc., 1997, pp. 69-73. Single or multiple copies of this article are available for a fee from The Haworth Document Delivery Service [1-800-342-9678, 9:00 a.m. - 5:00 p.m. (EST). E-mail address: getinfo@haworth.com].

69

when applying for and receiving disability benefits. Often symptoms of CFS, such as the fatigue or cognitive deficit, are not well understood by insurers, who take the position that a CFS sufferer can work in a sedentary position that allegedly does not require much physical or mental exertion. However, those who are truly familiar with CFS and its symptomatology know that the performance of even the simplest of tasks can have devastating physical and mental effects on the CFS sufferer.

LTD policies often apply an array of limitations on receiving payments of the LTD benefits. One of the most frequent is an imposed limitation on payment of LTD benefits for a certain period of time, frequently two years, for certain conditions. The limiting of payments of LTD benefits to two years for a *mental disorder* is very often contained within the LTD policy. Unfortunately, *mental disorder,* which is broadly interpreted by the insurer as including a wide spectrum of conditions, is often the label applied to persons suffering from CFS since there is currently no one definitive, objective test to confirm the diagnosis of CFS. Additionally, there is now an increasing trend for some insurers to draft policy language that expands the limitations on payments of benefits to clinically diagnosed conditions not "objectively" verifiable. This too may have the effect of limiting a CFS claimant from receiving benefits beyond a specified period of time.

CLAIMANTS ADMINISTRATIVE RECORD/CLAIM FILE

The documentation that the insurer reviews and uses to make a determination regarding the claimant's disability is contained in what is often referred to as either the *administrative record* or *claim file*. It is imperative that every bit of information that a claimant has or can obtain in support of his/her treating physician's diagnosis be submitted to be included in this file. Verify that the insurer has received the *complete* medical records from all of the treating and/or diagnosing physicians. The claimant should also obtain copies from these physicians and review them for accuracy and completeness. Occasionally records are not complete. It is extremely important that the records noting initial symptoms and documenting the onset of the illness are included. Again, it is imperative that the claimant's medical records be reviewed by the claimant and also by the treating physician for any information that may be incomplete, unclear, or could be misconstrued.

Because CFS is often a diagnosis based on reporting of symptoms by the patient and is further diagnosed by the exclusion of other illnesses, it is imperative that both the patient and his or her treating and diagnosing physicians carefully and thoroughly document every symptom, test, results of tests, results of examinations, any other findings, all treatments prescribed, and the results of these treatments. These records are going to be scrutinized by the insurer before determining (1) whether the claimant is disabled, and (2) what the *primary* cause of claimant's disability is.

It is extremely important when a patient is seen by a physician, or telephones the physician, that the records clearly document all relevant complaints and findings. If the patient had consistently complained of the fatigue every time he or she has seen the physician, then the records should reflect that. For example, the records of a patient seen by his or her treating physician on an ongoing basis for fatigue may not specify fatigue is reported at every visit. It may not seem necessary to the doctor to repeat this in the written notes at every visit that *every time the patient has been seen* that the patient has been suffering from fatigue. The doctor knows what he is seeing the patient for every other week, and the patient knows what she is seeing the doctor for every other week. However, if fatigue is *not specifically recorded in the medical records,* this becomes a glaring omission that the insurer may interpret to suggest the patient was not suffering from *ongoing fatigue* and therefore the diagnosis of CFS is incorrect.

It is also not uncommon to encounter references to psychological/psychiatric symptoms in CFS patient charts. One example would be encountering physician's notes indicating that the CFS patient is suffering from depression. Depression is often experienced by persons with CFS. However, if the medical charts and notes do not clearly and very specifically describe that this depression, or any other psychiatric symptom, is *secondary* to the CFS, the insurer may conclude that the claimant's disability is a result of a mental illness and *apply a mental illness time limitation of benefits being paid for only two years.*

There is also the need to specify what each medication is being prescribed for. Oftentimes anti-depressants are prescribed in the treatment of CFS but these medications are misconstrued by insurers as "evidence" that the patient is suffering from clinical depression.

The insurance company will scrutinize every report and bit of information in the patient's record and look for inaccuracies, inconsistencies and omissions. It is imperative that any such inaccuracy, inconsistency or omission be resolved prior to the insurance company's approving, denying, or limiting payment of the LTD benefits. This can be done by the patient's obtaining written documentation from the appropriate physician, resolving them, and submitting this information promptly to the insurance company.

The claimant should also submit whatever information he/she believes will assist the insurance company in approving his/her benefits. Testimonials from friends, clergy, and associates documenting how the claimant was prior to the onset of CFS and their observations of how the claimant is today are useful. If possible, the claimant should obtain testimonials from employers, preferably a supervising employer, documenting how the claimant's work performance was and is affected by CFS.

INSURER'S REVIEW
OF ADMINISTRATIVE RECORD/CLAIM FILE

The records submitted by the claimant are the records that the insurer is going to review, interpret, and base its determination on whether or not the claimant is (1) disabled, and (2) disabled from CFS and not some other condition. Further, these determinations are often made by non-medical personnel such as benefits analysts or claim representatives, who are not medically qualified to make a diagnosis of CFS. Their determinations are sometimes reviewed by a medically trained person, whether a nurse or physician, who is either on the staff of the insurance company or contracts with the insurance company to conduct these reviews. The insurer may also request that the claimant submit to an "Independent" Medical Examination ("IME") to confirm or rule out CFS. This examination may consist of a psychiatric evaluation with no physical examination, an examination by a physician specializing in rheumatology, etc. The examiner may not even believe in the existence of CFS. We encountered such a case where the psychiatrist did not believe CFS existed and thought it could be attributed to a psychiatric disorder. This was the person the insurance company hired to conduct the "*Independent* Medical Examination" of a claimant with CFS.

However, despite all of the documentation submitted on the claimant's behalf supporting the treating physician's diagnosis that the patient is suffering from CFS and is disabled as a result of the CFS, the LTD claim may still be denied or severely limited by the application of limitations such as a limit of two years of payments for a mental illness.

Further, it is not unusual for the insurer to investigate the claimant through the use of private investigators, public records, or surveillance, including video surveillance, to augment the administrative record/claim file.

CLAIM DENIED OR IMPOSE LIMITATIONS

Should the insurer deny the claim for LTD benefits or impose limitations on the payments of the LTD benefits, the claimant should immediately proceed with the remedies available to him/her. Some of these remedies, such as the right to request an administrative review of the decision, should be specified in the notice from the insurer. Of course the claimant has the right, *at any time during the pendency* of the LTD claim, to consult with an attorney regarding his/her LTD claim for benefits.

Perspectives on CFS and Impairment: Proposed Guidelines for Disability Determination

Donald Uslan, MA, MBA

SUMMARY. Chronic fatigue syndrome (CFS) is a difficult condition for which to determine work limitations and disability. This paper discusses the current problems in the state-of-the-art, and proposes framework standards for multi-disciplinary rehabilitation efforts to assess, prevent or limit disability, and multi-disciplinary standards for disability determination. *[Article copies available for a fee from The Haworth Document Delivery Service: 1-800-342-9678. E-mail address: getinfo@haworth.com]*

INTRODUCTION

The primary reason for a dialogue about disability guidelines for patients with a diagnosis of chronic fatigue syndrome (CFS) is to allow them a legitimate opportunity to procure financial coverage from insurers. Sec-

---

Donald Uslan is a National Certified Counselor, National Board for Certified Counselors (NCC), Certified Rehabilitation Counselor, Commission on Rehabilitation Counselor Certification (CRC), Diplomate, American Board of Disability Analysts (DABDA), Fellow, American Board of Medical Psychotherapists (FABMP), and Diplomate, American Board of Forensic Examiners (DABFE), Northwest Counseling Associations, Center for Comprehensive Care, 525 Minor Avenue, Seattle, WA 98104.

[Haworth co-indexing entry note]: "Perspectives on CFS and Impairment: Proposed Guidelines for Disability Determination." Uslan, Donald. Co-published simultaneously in *Journal of Chronic Fatigue Syndrome* (The Haworth Medical Press, an imprint of The Haworth Press, Inc.) Vol. 3, No. 4, 1997, pp. 75-85; and: *Disability and Chronic Fatigue Syndrome: Clinical, Legal and Patient Perspectives* (ed: Nancy G. Klimas, and Roberto Patarca) The Haworth Medical Press, an imprint of The Haworth Press, Inc., 1997, pp. 75-85. Single or multiple copies of this article are available for a fee from The Haworth Document Delivery Service [1-800-342-9678, 9:00 a.m. - 5:00 p.m. (EST). E-mail address: getinfo@haworth.com].

ondarily, health care professionals need to be able to assess and recommend limitations and restrictions in their patient's functioning in the context of their intervention and treatment with some degree of consistency and reliability. And, thirdly, those practitioners who are in the role of independent evaluators require reasonable standards and measures to determine impairment. Insurers are unable to fairly determine benefits without such standards, measures and guidelines. These do not uniformly exist at present.

Guidelines about disability need to be generated from the practitioner, patient, and researcher as well as the insurance communities. Recently, the health insurance industry has taken considerable flack about its limitation of coverage or restriction of services for a variety of high cost chronic medical conditions, even for those well understood and documented. Those insurers who do not act may find themselves acted upon. The U.S. Congress has even intervened to establish minimum acceptable insurance coverage hospital stays for new-baby deliveries, and the American Medical Association and the federal government have recommended basic standards for mammography in women over forty years old in order to counter a trend in reducing these services.

The managed care insurance movement has begun to cope with the public criticism of some of its limitations in services by turning to the various disease foundations, such as the Arthritis Foundation and the American Heart Association, for assistance with pre-established protocols as to what constitutes effective clinical intervention, basing their approval or denial of services based on these protocols.

DISCUSSION

The Problem

Disability can be a major issue in CFS (1,2). In the medical condition of fibromyalgia syndrome (FMS), with many clinical similarities to CFS, it is estimated that twenty-five percent of the patients seen in rheumatology practices receive disability benefits (3). However, the Social Security Administration has had difficulty in understanding how to approach CFS as a disabling condition, and has recently convened an advisory group of research, evaluation, practitioner, and patient advocate representatives from the CFS field to assist in refining its handling of determination of disability. Similarly, the private disability insurance field does not have the tools to evaluate or understand CFS (4).

There is now a spate of legal cases pitting disability insurers against patients attempting to receive long-term disability benefits. It appears insurers have difficulties establishing guidelines for a determination of CFS. Other medical conditions have a variety of markers and standards for understanding impairment. For example, breast cancer patients have ratings and recovery percentages, and cardiac patients are compared to a disability scale with severity levels of impairment. The field of workers' compensation physical injuries has a whole industry of impairment ratings. Measurements of range of motion and strength are used to arrive at a determination of total impairment as outlined by the American Medical Association Guide to the Evaluation of Permanent Impairment (5). However, these standards, when applied to CFS, indicate little or no impairment.

Some Current Determinants of Disability

Because of the as yet undetermined cause or causes of CFS, no "objective" markers exist to document a mutually acceptable means of definition. The possible multiple causes of CFS indicate it may not be a homogenous syndrome, making "objective" means of determining disability difficult. The tools often used to assist in the determination of disability are few and not necessarily reliable or consistently applied to CFS. If, in the future, objective measures using biological markers (such as immune abnormalities), standardized testing impairment ratings or other quantitative measurements become available, the acceptance of the "medical," "physical" or "biological" origins of CFS and the subsequent development of quantifiable standards for determination of disability will be more readily accepted by insurers.

In the meantime, the Social Security Administration (SSA), which has attempted to come to terms with CFS as a disabling medical condition, often uses its "mental impairments" standards, such as depression, to determine disability. The utilization of the mental impairment model allows the SSA to consider *functional impairments* in activities of daily living and occupational functioning more readily than the medical disease model. And, if a person does not meet the strict Center for Disease Control criteria for CFS due to some exclusionary condition, this model of functional impairment does not preclude acceptance of *chronic fatigue*, CF, as a disabling condition. Psychological and medical disabilities have no discrepancy in benefits for Social Security Administration programs. However, this paradigm ultimately involves using a DSM-IV (American Psychiatric Association's *Diagnostic and Statistic Manual IV*) diagnosis. Unless the accepted psychological condition is based on the accepted presence of CFS as a medical condition, this is offensive to many persons with CFS due to the implication of the psychological origins rather than the physical source of symptoms.

Conversely, the private long-term disability insurance industry typically has a limitation on any psychological condition versus life-time benefits for medical impairments. Many patients fear a Social Security determination of benefits based on "psychological" because of its potential limitations for a co-existing Long-term Disability claim, despite reassurance by the SSA that SSA files are sealed and unavailable to outside parties.

Independent Medical Examinations (IME's) typically do not function merely as a second opinion to the primary care physician or as a consultation to the insurer, but, rather, as an adversary under the guise of a medical evaluator. An IME may have two or three specialty physicians (typically an orthopedist or neurologist) who may have little or no applicability to chronic fatigue syndrome. The utilization of a psychiatric assessment can be problematic if the assessment is based on a series of non-objective symptoms representing somatic complaints, rather than on the medical validity of CFS. The utilization of the Minnesota Multiphasic Inventory (MMPI) can be problematic in the assessment of persons with chronic medical problems (6). Neuropsychological testing may not be effective in determining cognitive problems in terms of impairment.

Moreover, forms given physicians to sign and to document disability are frequently inadequate and/or unsuitable to CFS since such forms typically have been designed for musculo-skeletal injuries. These forms do not address the "flares" or cycles of fatigue and/or pain, variations in cognitive functioning and the need for physical accommodation. These forms may provide limited check-boxes indicating specific weight or weight categories the patient is able to lift and carry during the work day. Furthermore, physicians are asked to judge work ability or impairment, an area in which they typically are not trained (7).

Standards

A reasonable consensus of *standards of care* or *standards of rehabilitation or standards of disability* in CFS represents the best interests of all parties. Effective medical treatment, rehabilitation and determinations of disability minimize the management effort of providers, the time and waiting with consequential growing impairment by patients, administrative waste by payors, and the financial costs to insurers, providers and patients alike. It therefore behooves the CFS patient and professional community to fashion reasonable guidelines and work with payors to determine what patient profile, symptom constellation, criterion or response to intervention falls inside as well as outside the guidelines.

Proposal

Unfortunately, doubt and accusation as the intentions and motivations of the "stakeholders" (the interested parties) taint most attempts to creative constructive dialogue and progressive compromise. This reality notwithstanding, I believe the discussion should focus on two areas: *rehabilitation,* or the effort to prevent or "treat" the impairments of a person with CFS so that he or she will not need or minimally need to be considered unable to work; and *disability,* or the condition of a significantly impaired person who is no longer able to maintain gainful employment on a short-term or long-term basis. *Disability,* then, can only be considered after *rehabilitation* efforts have failed to prevent maintenance on the job or failed to return a CFS sufferer to the job, and these rehabilitation interventions serve to document and act as "objective" standards for the purposes of determining disability.

Rehabilitation

A legitimate effort at rehabilitation of persons with the condition of CFS needs to incorporate, in addition to medical work-ups, elements of the following. Debate and dialogue should attempt to prioritize and clarify which interventions are most efficacious (8). (This list is by no means exhaustive.)

- *Preventive Health:* ergonomics, safety assessment, employer training and consultation, provider training and education, health education.
- *Care Management:* community resources (access/referral/advocacy), patient training and education.
- *Natural Health Intervention:* acupuncture, naturopathy, chiropractic, biofeedback, herbal, massage, and nutrition/dietary treatment and intervention.
- *Psycho/Social Intervention:* medical conditions counseling, cognitive and functional therapies, vocational counseling, group/individual/family therapy, general psychotherapy, pain management, stress management, lifestyle adjustment counseling, addictions and chemical dependency treatment and counseling, career counseling, bibliotherapy, cognitive rehabilitation and support groups.
- *Physical Intervention (8):* physical therapy, postural alignment, spinal assessment and treatment, muscular conditioning, injury prevention and education.

- *Occupational Intervention (8):* occupational therapy, job site assessment and modification, daily living skills, adaptive therapies, working hardening/conditioning, vocational counseling, return to work interventions, home access and safety assessment, environmental assessment and planning.

Disability

Impairment and disability cannot be determined in CFS by physical or chemical testing. Impairment or disability relative to work and personal activities of daily living (ADL) functioning may be determined by subjective report, professional assessment and/or "objective" performance in testing and evaluation in the work place. Thus, key criteria for determination of impairment or disability are: the credibility of the patient based on his or her accuracy and validity as an historian; determination of psychological sequelae; objective performance such as work history and performance based physical capacity evaluation; efforts to remain at work and return to work after onset; co-worker and employer assessment; and the use of professional health care provider judgment based on experience with a patient over a period of time and in conjunction with a comparison to other patients presenting with similar features.

The following are guidelines by the federal government for the determination of government employee disability benefits:

- A deficiency in occupational functioning with respect to performance, conduct, or attendance, or, in the absence of any actual occupational deficiency, a demonstration that the medical condition is incompatible with either useful service or retention in the patient's position;
- A medical condition, which is defined as a disease or injury;
- A relationship between the occupational deficiency and the medical condition indicating the medical condition has caused the occupational deficiency;
- The duration of the medical condition, both past and expected, and a substantiation that the condition, in all probability, will continue to be disabling for at least one year;
- The patient's inability to perform useful and efficient service arose while the employee was serving under the employer;
- The inability of the employer to make reasonable accommodation to the employee's medical condition;
- The absence of another available position to which the employee is qualified for reassignment.

Disability Evaluation Components

Evaluations should be performed by licensed and/or certified providers working within the domain and scope of their professional practice and licensure who have been trained in the criteria, etiology, history, treatment alternatives for conditions such as CFS using standardized protocols:

Medical (9)

Standardized medical evaluation to include the following:
- diagnosis/diagnoses
- utilization of specialty medical consultation
- diagnostics and laboratory procedures as necessary to substantiate diagnoses and for consideration of pharmacologic or other interventions
- utilization of a consensus report form or format for physicians to sign and document their assessment which is specifically designed for CFS

Psychiatric Evaluation

- Rule in/out exclusionary psychiatric conditions to diagnosis of CFS;
- Determine psychiatric conditions, if any;
- Assess efficacy of medications, including hypnotics;
- Determine co-morbidity of psychiatric and medical conditions;
- Rule in/out somatoform disorders;
- Evaluate potential of psychotherapeutic interventions to assist in medical/psychiatric coping;
- Recommend type of therapeutic intervention;
- Establish psychiatric interview baseline for future reference;
- Neuropsychological consultation and objective evaluation as necessary to determine cognitive deficits (including general academic and intellectual ability, attention, reasoning, numerical processing, abstract thinking, response execution, executive function, memory, judgment, personality and mood states) (6)

Occupational Therapy Evaluation (6)

- Daily activity; self-care; household chores; yard work; car maintenance; shopping; recreation; exercise; rest periods; adaptive equipment; pacing strategies

Performance-Based Physical Capacity Evaluations (6)

- Subjective complaints: description of results of injury/illness; areas of discomfort; description of discomfort; increase in symptoms; decrease in symptoms; devices
- Objective data: range of motion/lower extremities; straight leg raising; range of motion/upper extremities; cervical range of motion
- Cardiopulmonary exercise endurance testing
- Isokenetic Limb Testing: gait evaluation/physiology; grip strength/grip span/maximum voluntary effort testing
- Other observations: vision screening; communication skills; cognitive abilities; attitude and behavior; body mechanics
- Conclusion: validity; consistency; specific involved area; general strength; physiology; adaptation to employment activities; comparisons to norms; overall deficit; motion restrictions
- Recommendations: level of work activity; part-time/full-time; remedial programs; adaptive equipment

Vocational Evaluation

Typically, a vocational rehabilitation evaluation forms conclusions which address, demonstrate and document the following, utilizing job descriptions, job analyses and other job characteristics:

- Based on the patient's age, physical or medical status, geographical location, local labor market, education and background, and transferable work skills, does he possess the ability to enter the competitive labor market;
- If he or she is able to enter the competitive labor market, and, if so, in what capacity (part- or full-time);
- Potential specific possible occupational options;
- Initial plan of rehabilitation to assist the individual to return to gainful employment;
- Outline of costs for rehabilitation and return-to-work;
- Other potential interventions to assist rehabilitation and return-to-work.

A comprehensive vocational rehabilitation evaluation supports the above conclusions by outlining the following categories (sub-categories are suggestions):

- *Identifying Information:* referral information; reason for referral.
- *Medical/Health:* health history based on records review and primary health care provider communication (current health, current symptoms,

medications, current medications, allergies); chemical addictions; providers; current treatments; fatigue scale; sleep/rest; pain levels; activity level.

- *Rehabilitation Considerations:* psychosocial history; legal involvement; activities of daily living (past and present); driving and drivers' license; current interests; hobbies; activities; transportation.
- *Vocational Factors:* education and training; work history (employer, job title, dates of employment, DOT [*Dictionary of Occupational Titles*] title, DOT code); military experience; occupational analysis; summary of occupational history factors (combined work history); specific vocational preparation (SVP); general educational development (GED); strength (physical requirements); working conditions (environment); work situations (temperaments); DOT aptitudes; work functions (data-people-things).
- *Rehabilitation Implications:* subjective; physician opinions; provider opinions; independent evaluations; character and personal statements; performance evaluations.
- *Objective Measures:* work history; return-to-work efforts; testing; performance based physical capacity evaluation.
- *Rehabilitation Assessments; Scales and Ratings* (vocational expert's professional assessments): critical behavioral factors in rehabilitation; global assessment of functioning; impairment severity; severity of psychosocial stressors scale; functional limitations; mental/nervous impairment; physical impairment (as defined in the U.S. Department of Labor's *Dictionary of Occupational Titles*); residual functional capacity assessment (mental impairment); work/social restriction level; barriers to employment; assets to employment or rehabilitation; past relevant work summary–(1. physical demands [exertion level]–2. physical requirements–3. skill level: specific vocational preparation [SVP]).
- *Conclusions and Opinions:* definitive statements, based on the above foundations, of the person's impairments and ability to work; rehabilitation planning for returning to work; strategies for staying at work; deficiencies in treatment interventions which may impact workability; feasibility assessment and proposals for accommodation and modification of job or work station; and other pragmatic approaches to assist patient with maximal occupational functioning.

CONCLUSION

In recent years, more attention has been given to treatment models of care and functional assessment of CFS, but the process of disability determination for patient applicants with CFS remains inadequate, sluggish, and sometimes even unfair and inhumane. In determining disability, a consensus on standardized reporting forms and the establishment of requirements for minimal levels of expertise for evaluators of disability are essential. Critical issues in treatment and rehabilitation preliminary to assessment of impairment, as well as disability standards and protocols, must be reviewed, reevaluated, and resolved. The utilization of objective measures such as functional evaluations, neuropsychological testing and exercise endurance testing need to be incorporated into a professional vocational assessment of ability to work. Only through such measures can a standard of evaluation endorsed by the CFS community and acceptable to the disability insurance industry be achieved.

ACKNOWLEDGMENTS

The author acknowledges the assistance of Virginia Teague, MA. The author would also like to thank Dedra Buchwald, MD, and Phalla Kith, PA, of the Chronic Fatigue Clinic at the University of Washington, Seattle, WA, and Pamela Webb Driscoll, RN, BSN, of the Center for Comprehensive Care, Seattle, WA.

REFERENCES

1. Komaroff AL, Fagioli LR, et al. Health status in patients with chronic fatigue syndrome and in general population and disease comparison groups. *Am J Med* 1996; 101(3): 281-290.

2. Bombardier CH, Buchwald D. Chronic Fatigue, Chronic fatigue syndrome, and fibromyalgia. Disability and health-care use. *Med Care* 1996; 34(9): 924-930.

3. Wrenn F. CFS and disability. *The CFIDS Chronicle* 1997; 10(1): 61-63.

4. Wolfe F, Aarflot T. et al. Fibromyalgia and disability. *Scand J Rheumatol* 1995; 24: 112-8.

5. Bennett R. Editorial–Disabling Fibromyalgia: Appearance Versus Reality. *The Journal of Rheumatology.* 1993; 20(1): 1821-1822.

6. Barrows D. Functional capacity evaluations of persons with chronic fatigue immune dysfunction syndrome. *Am J of Occupational Therapy* 1995; 49(4): 327-337.

7. Heiman T. Chronic fatigue syndrome and vocational rehabilitation: unserved and unmet needs. *J of Chronic Fatigue Syndrome* 1995; 1(3/4): 105-118.

8. Hicks J. General approaches to the rehabilitation in chronic fatigue syndrome. *J of Chronic Fatigue Syndrome* 1995; 1(3/4): 85-90.

9. Salit I. et al. Chronic Fatigue Syndrome: A Position Paper. *J of Rheum* 1966; 23(3): 540-543.

SUGGESTED READING

Buchwald D, Pearlman T, Umali J, Schmaling K, Katon W. Functional status in patients with chronic fatigue syndrome, other fatiguing illnesses, and healthy individuals. *Am J Med* 1996; 101(4): 364-370.

Ehrlich G, Wolfe F. On the difficulties of disability and its determination. *Rheum Disease Clinics of North America* 1996; 22(3): 613.

Wolfe F, Potter J. Fibromyalgia and work disability: is fibromyalgia a disabling disorder? *Rheum Clinics of North Am* 1996; 22(2): 369.

THE PATIENT'S PERSPECTIVE

Long-Term Disability:
Long-Term Deception?

"Annie Bloom"

In recent years, hundreds of persons with CFIDS (PWCs) have described the problems they have encountered while trying to obtain long-term disability (LTD) benefits from private, for-profit insurance companies. For these PWCs, the glowing promises of security and support tucked into their disability insurers' colorful marketing pamphlets faded quickly when they presented claims supported by a CFIDS diagnosis. Even the nation's most profitable disability insurers failed to honor their

Some material from this article has been adapted from a previous article titled "Delays, Denials and Deceptions: The Truth About LTD Insurance" by Annie Bloom, published in *The CFIDS Chronicle*, Vol. 9, No. 4 (Fall 1996), pages 25-34. It is used here with permission of The CFIDS Association of America, Inc., P.O. Box 220398, Charlotte, NC 28222-0398.

The author has requested anonymity and has therefore used a pseudonym.

Address correspondence to: Virginia Teague, Managing Editor, *Journal of Chronic Fatigue Syndrome*, 600 Krohn Court, Irving, TX 75038.

[Haworth co-indexing entry note]: "Long-Term Disability: Long-Term Deception?" 'Bloom, Annie.' Co-published simultaneously in *Journal of Chronic Fatigue Syndrome* (The Haworth Medical Press, an imprint of The Haworth Press, Inc.) Vol. 3, No. 4, 1997, pp. 87-97; and: *Disability and Chronic Fatigue Syndrome: Clinical, Legal and Patient Perspectives* (ed: Nancy G. Klimas, and Roberto Patarca) The Haworth Medical Press, an imprint of The Haworth Press, Inc., 1997, pp. 87-97. Single or multiple copies of this article are available for a fee from The Haworth Document Delivery Service [1-800-342-9678, 9:00 a.m. - 5:00 p.m. (EST). E-mail address: getinfo@haworth.com].

87

pledge to provide prompt and careful review of completed applications; reward cooperative claimants with faster service; issue benefit checks every month to claimants who satisfied the provisions of their policies; offer skilled assistance with Social Security claims; and help claimants deal effectively with the many aspects of disability. In contrast, nearly all PWCs reported being subjected to frustrating delays, unfair denials, or abrupt terminations; many also endured harassment, mendacity, and invasions of their privacy by the insurers' employees.

Although my own illness prevents me from constructing a scientific survey of claims handling practices, the picture that emerges from extensive contacts with other PWCs is clear: after enduring years of distortions and deceit, most regard their disability insurers as adversaries, not allies.[1]

The oldest, poorest, sickest and most trusting PWCs are singled out for the worst abuses by insurance company employees who accuse them of being lazy, badger them to return to work, and lie to them about the terms of their policies. Insurers take advantage of their physical frailty and financial distress to pressure these claimants to accept absurdly small settlements, relinquish their rights to future benefits, and agree not to discuss their settlements, while denying them time to obtain adequate legal counsel.

Even those PWCs who receive benefits feel that they have paid an enormous price for the income replacement promised in their policies. Many depleted their savings to retain skilled attorneys and obtain state-of-the-art medical documentation to support their claims, while enduring invasive scrutiny by physicians and investigators hired by the insurer. Those whose LTD policies were provided by employers were denied important legal protections against deceitful practices by their insurers and had to satisfy an especially rigorous standard to prove their claims. These claimants live with the abiding fear that their hard-won benefits will abruptly and unjustly be taken away.

While claims for CFIDS represent only about one or two percent of the total volume of disability claims filed in the U.S. and Canada each year,[2] the rapid increase in the number of these claims and the prolonged period for which claimants are incapacitated have prompted disability insurers to take increasingly aggressive steps to limit the unwelcome financial liability created by this devastating illness. In response, PWCs are beginning to share information in order to identify the primary obstacles to securing LTD benefits. With support from their national organizations and access to the Internet, PWCs are developing strategies to promote fairer handling of LTD claims by a powerful industry which has shown more concern for increasing profits than providing the protections pledged to their disabled claimants. In the following pages, the principal problems encountered by PWCs filing long-term disability claims will be examined and some possible remedies will be proposed.

Prolonged, excessive and stressful delays during the processing of CFIDS claims leave PWCs without funds needed to meet financial obligations and provide subsistence for themselves and their families. They may also be unable to pay for treatment by medical specialists who understand their illness or retain skilled attorneys to assist them with their claims. It is not unusual for claimants to wait from six months to a year before a final decision is made by the insurer to pay or deny the claim. During this period of increasing uncertainty and financial stress, claimants may deplete their savings and retirement funds; witness the decimation of their credit ratings; and face bankruptcies, foreclosures, and evictions from their homes. Some patients, suffering from an illness which many still deny is real, lose respect and support from their closest friends and family members during this prolonged period of insolvency. For most PWCs, the stress of dealing with long delays, harassment by claims personnel, and mounting financial concerns can exacerbate symptoms and jeopardize opportunities for improvement or recovery.

While the specific strategies employed by insurers to delay decisions on CFIDS claims vary, a predictable sequence of communications with insurers usually follows submission of a claim. The first acknowledgment promises a response within 60 days; however, the response is not a decision, but a request for another 60 days to process the claim. At the end of four months, claimants may be told their claim has been sent to the insurer's medical department, leaving the acutely ill CFIDS patient to wonder what, if anything, was done during the tense months of waiting for payments to begin.

After more weeks pass without news from the insurer, some claimants initiate a frustrating sequence of phone calls (unanswered), faxes (lost), and letters (misplaced) to the benefits specialist handling the claim. Additional reasons given for delays include misplacing records (1 month); locating a doctor for an independent medical examination (IME) (2 months); and waiting for the IME report (another 2 months). Employees of a company that boasts being "First in Premium Dollars" tell claimants that the doctor reviewing their claims only comes in one day a week, and there is a backlog of claims ahead of theirs. Thus, an acutely ill claimant can be kept waiting without funds for a year before a decision is made on the PWCs claim.

The problems created by these delays could be mitigated by requiring insurers to begin paying claims as soon as the elimination period has ended and a licensed physician has certified that the claimant is disabled and unable to work under the terms of the insured's policy. Denied claimants would not have to repay amounts received while the insurer processed their claims unless the insurer can prove fraud.

The absence of consistent standards for evaluating CFIDS claims suggests that insurers may be more interested in assessing the PWC's ability to challenge a denial than in making fair and medically-defensible determinations of eligibility for benefits. Five PWCs who applied for benefits from the same insurer reported remarkable differences in the way their claims were handled. The first was told that the insurer would not pay any benefits for CFIDS. The next two were told that CFIDS was not a valid medical diagnosis; what they really had was depression. One of the "depressed" claimants was paid benefits for two years on the basis of mental illness; the other was told her claim would be dragged out for years unless she immediately accepted a very small settlement. The fourth claimant's physician received a letter discussing the current CDC criteria for diagnosing CFIDS. The fifth PWC, employed by an influential law firm and covered by a policy which did not limit benefits for mental illness, submitted medical evidence comparable to that provided by the other four claimants and has received payments for her CFIDS claim for several years.

A former claims manager reported that his company routinely denied all CFIDS claims the first time they were filed, then waited to see which claimants would appeal. Another insurance company employee was told that no CFIDS claim would be paid beyond two years unless the claimant hired an attorney. Many PWCs who satisfy both the 1988 and 1994 CDC criteria for CFIDS, and who have successfully obtained Social Security Disability Insurance on the basis of CFIDS, continue to be denied benefits or labeled mentally ill by their LTD insurers. Most PWCs are denied benefits at least once because they have not provided "objective evidence of disability." However, when asked what additional evidence is needed to perfect their claims, insurers will not disclose this vital information.

LTD insurers demand that claimants provide irrefutable, objective evidence of disability to establish their claims. However, evidence used by insurers to deny claims is not subjected to the rigorous scrutiny which reports from claimants' physicians must endure. Claimants who believe that board certified physicians determine their eligibility for benefits may be surprised to learn that decisions are made by claims representatives or managers with minimal training. Their sophisticated and costly medical evidence will probably be reviewed by an insurance company nurse. A former claims manager admitted that medical information is usually not reviewed by a doctor "unless the insurer feels threatened in some way." Attorneys who challenge denied CFIDS claims confirm that nurses write the detailed comments found in claimants' medical files, with company doctors simply initialing the nurses' conclusions.

The qualifications and medical experience of nurses and doctors employed by the insurer are unknown to claimants, and they may be grossly unsuited to diagnose patients who present complex, multi-systemic, new and emerging medical conditions. Yet any doctor employed by an insurance company can refute the judgments of a panel of nationally-recognized CFIDS experts and the claim will be denied. Courts have even upheld such decisions as legitimate differences of medical opinion and ruled against claimants.

It is imperative that LTD insurers (and the Social Security Administration) establish consistent guidelines for providing proof of claim for CFIDS. These guidelines should be grounded in current medical knowledge and diagnostic criteria determined by the CDC, and provided promptly upon request to claimants, physicians, and attorneys.

Many LTD policies include discriminatory time limits for specific diagnoses, such as mental illness, chronic fatigue syndrome, or "self-reported" conditions.

Once a CFIDS patient has presented convincing evidence of disability, or demonstrated the determination and resources to continue pursuing the claim, insurance company employees may attempt to classify the claimant's condition as "mental or nervous" in order to limit benefits to the 24-months provided for these conditions in most LTD policies. As many as 50% of those who claim benefits for CFIDS are at some time labeled mentally ill,[3] often by an on-site physician employed by the insurer who has never seen the claimant and whose identity and qualifications are unknown. Those most likely to be steered into this classification include claimants who are women; have already received benefits for several years; or whose policies were acquired by the insurer through a merger or acquisition. If medical records document such common CFIDS correlates as depression, anxiety, panic attacks, psychotherapy, or use of antidepressants to relieve symptoms, the insurer may insist that the claimant's primary condition is "psychological," ignoring pages of medical evidence supporting a physical basis for the claimant's disability. Insurers have also abused the highly restrictive screening criteria developed for research purposes by insisting that the presence of any past or current psychiatric diagnosis or history of substance abuse precludes a finding of CFIDS. Some claimants recently classified "mentally ill" by their insurers have been required to submit evidence of ongoing psychotherapy, a treatment plan, and return to work goals in order to receive the limited disability benefits available for this condition.

If the insured's policy does not contain limitations for mental/nervous conditions, the insurer may insist that the claimant's subjective symptoms do not provide objective evidence of disability. In July, 1996, the Wall Street Journal reported that disability insurers are taking aggressive steps to limit or deny benefits for CFIDS and other conditions for which there is currently no objective lab test, x-ray, or diagnostic marker that can conclusively determine the presence of illness and the claimant's degree of disability.[4] Many companies are writing new and renewal policies with 12 or 24 month lifetime limits on benefits for these "self-reported" conditions. Some insurers offer substantial discounts to employers who replace more liberal policies with "budget" coverage limiting benefits for CFIDS and other "self-reported" conditions to only one year, and then blame employers for imposing the new limits. A pioneering Silicon Valley corporation, known for its benevolent treatment of employees, offers generous accommodations to disabled employees who are well enough to continue working, but imposes a one-year limit on disability benefits for CFIDS or Fibromyalgia.

A recent appellate court decision in New York challenges the practice of denying claims for lack of objective medical evidence where there is no definitive marker for an illness. The Third Circuit Court of Appeals affirmed the ruling of a lower court that denial of disability benefits to an employee with chronic fatigue syndrome because the claimant couldn't prove the cause of his condition violated ERISA, a complex body of laws that governs retirement plans and other employee benefits. The court noted that there is no "dipstick test" for the syndrome, and ruled that the employer's denial of benefits because the employee failed to show objective medical evidence of total disability was "arbitrary and capricious" since the cause of CFIDS is unknown.[5]

Advocates for the rights of disabled persons are seeking parity in health care for the mentally ill and have challenged limits on LTD benefits for mental illness under the Americans with Disabilities Act (ADA).[6] The Equal Employment Opportunity Commission (EEOC) has asserted that it is improper to differentiate between mental and physical illness in LTD policies. In Massachusetts, a PWC recently introduced new legislation to ban discriminatory insurance products in her state.[7] After the bill received a positive response from many legislators, the insurance lobby began taking steps to curtail the measure.

Joining coalitions with other disability rights organizations to support similar state and federal legislation may help us eliminate discriminatory time limits imposed for specific diagnoses, such as mental illness, chronic fatigue syndrome, or "self-reported" conditions and challenge the practice of cutting rates on employer-provided policies which provide inferior protection for employees afflicted by these conditions.

Decisions on claims are often based on "independent" medical examinations performed by unqualified, biased, or unscrupulous examiners selected and compensated by insurers. Independent medical examinations (IMEs) are frequently used by insurers to rebut medical evidence of disability provided by claimants' own physicians. Examiners may be screened to determine their willingness to provide the conclusions needed by the insurer. Several PWCs were required to travel to locations substantial distances from their homes for these examinations, despite the availability of qualified physicians nearby. Others were sent to examiners who admitted knowing nothing about CFIDS or insisted that CFIDS was not a legitimate diagnosis.

A few claimants found correspondence in their files indicating that the IME doctor's conclusions had been changed and evidence of disability suppressed at the request of the insurer. A psychologist who attributed a claimant's disability to mental illness changed his diagnosis to malingering after the insurer pointed out that the claimant's policy did not contain the usual limit on benefits for mental illness. A former athlete's performance on an exercise tolerance test was so dangerously abnormal that the procedure had to be stopped after only three minutes; yet the final IME report contained no indication that such a test had even been performed.

Any reasonable person would expect an independent medical examination of a PWC to be performed by a physician who is qualified to recognize and diagnose CFIDS, and who has enough experience treating PWCs to reliably assess the claimant's degree of disability and prospects for improvement. The establishment of a national registry of qualified, ethical, and impartial experts familiar with current medical standards for diagnosis and treatment of the condition being evaluated, along with a panel to review complaints challenging the qualifications and impartiality of these examiners, is needed to protect claimants from fraudulent IMEs.

Insurers use the protection afforded them by ERISA to delay and deny payment of claims with impunity. PWCs with the physical, mental, and monetary resources to challenge their denied claims often spend thousands of dollars and years of their lives fighting a formidable and ruthless adversary shielded by a nearly impermeable legal fortress which neither Congress nor the Courts have been willing to attack. All claimants should receive equal treatment and protection under the law. However, the multibillion dollar insurance industry is protected by a pair of 1987 U.S. Supreme Court decisions that greatly restrict the relief available to claimants in cases where disability insurance is provided by an employer. Employee benefits, including group LTD insurance, fall under the jurisdiction of the Employee Retirement Income Security Act of 1974 (ERISA), a complex body of laws intended to protect employee benefits.[8] Ironically, these laws were created with the intent to simplify proceedings so that ordinary working people could be spared the expense of prolonged litigation in resolving disputes over their pension, health and welfare benefits. Two Supreme Court decisions in 1987 required ERISA cases to be tried in federal courts and limited awards to the amount of the benefits available under the contract of insurance, and, in some cases, the plaintiff's attorneys fees. Under ERISA, insurance companies cannot be held liable for bad faith, no matter how egregious their conduct is in denying claims. Thus, claimants whose employers provided their LTD policies, even if the employee paid all or part of the premium, are denied important protections which are available to claimants who purchase individual policies.

Many attorneys are reluctant to handle ERISA claims or require large retainers because they are usually difficult, prolonged, and yield very limited financial recovery due to claimants' inability to sue for compensatory or punitive damages. Thus, insurers believe they have little to lose by continuing to delay decisions on CFIDS claims; denying claimants who satisfy CDC criteria for CFIDS and SSDI criteria for disability; and bullying patients who are too sick to fight back.

The fact that ERISA contains a provision expressly stating that it completely preempts all state law on the substantive issues relating to these matters indicates that Congress considered that providing an alternative forum justified the preclusion of all state causes of action, including bad faith lawsuits for which compensatory and punitive damages could be awarded. In view of the unfortunate experiences already detailed, the argument has been advanced that the law is not working de facto (in reality) the way Congress intended, thus the courts should permit the state causes of action allowing claimants to recover damages. However, it is not the role of the courts to create legislation, but merely to interpret it. The court will instead state in its decision that it thinks the law is not working, and will urge the legislature to redraft or amend it. Therefore, the best relief for these abuses may lie in directing efforts toward encouraging Congress to reform ERISA.

Members of Congress who sympathize with working people have tried for years to reform ERISA laws, but have been blocked by partisan political alignments and the influence of the powerful insurance lobby. Perhaps the greatest possibility for securing more equitable treatment of CFIDS claims lies in exposing the fraudulent behavior of insurers who continue to deny claims despite substantial medical evidence of disability.

An ERISA reform bill currently in Congress which would grant members of HMOs the right to sue for punitive damages in malpractice suits would be an appropriate model for the type of legislation that is needed to allow persons with employer-provided long-term disability policies to receive the same treatment under the law as those who purchase their own income-replacement insurance. Such legislation would provide all claimants with equal protections against abusive treatment by making insurers liable for compensatory and punitive damages in cases where the insurer has acted in bad faith.

LTD insurers are intentionally defrauding PWCs by implementing special policies for handling CFIDS claims and making claims decisions that promote the insurer's financial interests instead of protecting legitimately disabled claimants. Many PWCs have complained that decisions on well-documented claims are intentionally prolonged for years in order to exhaust and bankrupt claimants, and soften their resistance to inadequate settlement offers. Others have objected to signing overly broad release of information forms which permit access to the claimant's most sensitive personal information, including all medical, psychiatric, substance abuse, employment, financial and credit information, to any person designated by the insurer. After being subjected to weeks of continuous surveillance, some PWCs faced immediate termination of their benefits based on a few seconds of videotape. PWCs have also been denied benefits following functional capacity evaluations which did not take into consideration the waxing and waning of CFIDS symptoms and the prolonged periods of post-exertional malaise that can follow a single day's efforts. The only PWC who reported receiving substantial assistance with a Social Security claim from his LTD insurer discovered that his LTD benefits were terminated immediately after the LTD insurer recovered close to $50,000 from his initial Social Security award. The LTD insurer then sent a surveillance video used to justify closing the claim to the office handling his Social Security benefits.

An internal document prepared for a major disability insurer by a staff physician characterizes CFIDS as "neurosis with a new banner" and outlines an aggressive plan to minimize "millions in potential losses from these claims." Features of this plan include winning the trust of physicians who treat PWCs and involving them in collaborative strategies to send claimants back to work; reviewing CFIDS claims every one to three months; and replicating the plan for all other "subjective" conditions.

One insurer implemented an aggressive disability management program using employees at the company's headquarters office as subjects. All workers on disability leave, including those convalescing from childbirth, heart attacks, and major surgery, were subjected to daily telephone calls from coworkers pressuring them to return to work immediately, despite not being released by their physicians. This program succeeded in creating a climate of intolerance for all disability claims managed by the insurer, and may account for the willingness of claims representatives to lie to CFIDS patients and harass those who are unable to go back to work. The same insurer has added disability management programs to its line of disability insurance products to help employers recognize the "hidden" costs of disability and take assertive measures to prevent the financial losses that occur when their employees file disability claims.

Insurers also provide substantial incentives for employees to deny claims. Competition within one company was encouraged by rewarding employees of the disability unit that closed the most claims. In 1996, the nation's largest disability insurer provided $18 million in bonuses to its employees through a "results sharing" program based on year-end profits.[9] Ambitious managers with aspirations for faster advancement and larger bonuses try to help the company save money by closing disability claims.

PWCs are already reporting more aggressive handling of their claims. Some report being surveilled around the time of an IME or home visit; a few were terminated if their level of activity did not match what they told the insurer's investigator. Claims are being reviewed more frequently, and some physicians have been required to submit treatment plans and establish return to work goals. Doctors who are also PWCs with active disability claims have experienced particularly abusive treatment from insurers who once considered their individual disability policies the most profitable segment of their business.[10] Now the same insurers who once courted their business are expending sizable sums to investigate and close these costly claims.

Operating in a highly competitive marketplace, with an economic climate driven by a fever for ever-increasing profits, many of the nation's leading insurance companies have forgotten their fiduciary duty to act "solely in the interest of the participants and beneficiaries"[11] by honoring their pledge to replace income lost due to serious and prolonged disability. In view of the substantial evidence of deceptive and fraudulent practices which has been provided by PWCs from all over the U.S., an immediate Congressional investigation into claims handling practices by long-term disability insurers is clearly warranted.

NOTES

1. For a detailed description of long-term disability claims handling practices, please refer to my article, "Delays, Denials and Deceptions: The Truth about LTD Insurance," in the Fall, 1996 issue of the CFIDS Chronicle.

2. Representatives of major insurers in the U.S. and Canada estimate that CFIDS accounts for approximately one to two percent of the total volume of their long-term disability claims.

3. This figure is based on the author's informal survey of 75 PWCs who filed disability claims and could provide copies of correspondence from insurers indicating the mental illness classification.

4. Jeffrey, Nancy Ann: Insurers curb some benefits for disability. The Wall Street Journal, vol. cxxxv no. 18 July 25, 1996.

5. U.S. COURT of Appeals, 3rd Circuit, Mitchell v. Eastman Kodak, 96-7034, May 8, 1997.

6. The protections for disabled persons available under the ADA also apply to persons who are perceived as having a disability, e.g., being labeled "mentally ill" by an insurer.

7. The full text of this bill is available in the Insurance Reform section of the WECAN website at http://www.community-care.org.uk/wecan/.

8. Claimants employed by the government or religious institutions, like those who purchase individual LTD policies, are exempted from ERISA and may sue for damages against LTD insurers in state courts.

9. Strosnider, Kim: UNUM workers share bonus. Portland Press Herald, Saturday, February 10, 1996.

10. Strosnider, Kim: Too many claims. Maine Sunday Telegram, Sunday, March 5, 1995.

11. 1996 Supreme Court ruling [Varity Corporation v. Howe, 116 S.Ct. 1065, 1074 (1996)].

Negotiating the Maze
of Disability Insurance:
One Patient's Perspective

Anonymous

It is no secret that people with chronic fatigue syndrome (CFS) find it difficult to get their claims for employer-provided long-term disability (LTD) benefits approved. This is rarely because they are not disabled. Rather, the current legal and medical climate creates unnecessary barriers to a fair and reasonable consideration of their claims. LTD insurance provided as an employee benefit is covered by a law originally intended to protect pension benefits, the Employee Retirement Income Security Act of 1974 (ERISA) (1). As applied to LTD claims, this law provides an incentive for insurance companies to drag out the claims process by any means possible since current Supreme Court interpretation of ERISA precludes state law claims for consequential damages (e.g., financial loss or emotional distress) as well as punitive damages (for, e.g., "bad faith"–the willful failure to honor contractual obligations) (2,3). The actions of several key federal agencies concerning CFS also have an impact on LTD claims. Unless the Centers for Disease Control (CDC) seriously investigate the epidemiology of this illness and publish up-to-date prevalence data and the National Institutes of Health (NIH) fund studies which compare CFS with similarly disabling diseases such as lupus and multiple sclerosis

The author has requested anonymity.

Address correspondence to: Virginia Teague, Managing Editor, *Journal of Chronic Fatigue Syndrome*, 600 Krohn Court, Irving, TX 75038.

[Haworth co-indexing entry note]: "Negotiating the Maze of Disability Insurance: One Patient's Perspective." Anonymous. Co-published simultaneously in *Journal of Chronic Fatigue Syndrome* (The Haworth Medical Press, an imprint of The Haworth Press, Inc.) Vol. 3, No. 4, 1997, pp. 99-109; and: *Disability and Chronic Fatigue Syndrome: Clinical, Legal and Patient Perspectives* (ed: Nancy G. Klimas, and Roberto Patarca) The Haworth Medical Press, an imprint of The Haworth Press, Inc., 1997, pp. 99-109. Single or multiple copies of this article are available for a fee from The Haworth Document Delivery Service [1-800-342-9678, 9:00 a.m. - 5:00 p.m. (EST). E-mail address: getinfo@haworth.com].

(stratifying research subjects by illness severity), LTD insurers will continue to believe that any CFS claim is lacking in credibility. Inconsistent and uninformed decisions by the Social Security Agency (SSA) in CFS-based Social Security Disability Insurance (SSDI) claims contribute to LTD carriers' dismissive attitude toward CFS.

The handling of my claim for disability benefits is an example of how the present medical and legal environment works against a genuinely disabled applicant. Disability insurers operating as employee benefit plans are required, by law, at a minimum, to handle claims in a manner that is not arbitrary and capricious.[1] This generally means their decisions must be reasonable and based on substantial evidence to be upheld in court. However, there are many ways to delay, harass, and intimidate without actually denying a claim. While some actions can be considered constructive denials, giving in to the insurer's demands is often the lesser of two evils compared to engaging in lengthy litigation.

It took several months of decreasing ability to perform my job due to what I thought was an unusually severe and persistent flu accompanied by odd headaches and cognitive problems before I sought out a physician nationally-renowned for his diagnostic skills. This doctor diligently considered every diagnosis imaginable with the assistance of specialists at a major medical center. During this extensive investigation, my condition deteriorated. It became apparent to both of us that I could no longer work. (I had tried my best to continue working as long as I could. As I became sicker, I cut back on my hours. Eventually, I became so functionally impaired I could barely get to the office.) Despite these problems, I simply could not imagine not working and I had a difficult time conceptualizing "disability." However, my doctor explained that my inability to work along with my difficulties with self-care did, indeed, "disable" me.

I reluctantly reviewed my LTD plan. Once I read its definition of disability, I felt I clearly met the plan's requirements. Still, it was with a heavy heart that I finally filed an application for benefits. My physician filled out his part of the form and added a letter. He described his extensive search to date for other diagnoses which could explain my illness and included the results of preliminary screening tests, some of which were abnormal. In addition, he documented how my symptoms affected my ability to work. While noting that there were signs that I might be developing another illness (something that would become clear only with further evaluation), he tentatively diagnosed my condition as CFS.

I fully expected that a favorable decision on my claim would be made in a timely manner. Three months after I filed my application for benefits, I finally received my insurer's decision. While this may, and did, feel like an extensive amount of time, under ERISA's accompanying regulations, the plan was allowed to render its decision up to 90 days after receipt of my claim (4). The decision was a denial of benefits. Even though the CDC had categorically stated in its 1988 working case definition of CFS (5) that there was no diagnostic test for the illness, my denial was based in part on there being "no substantiating objective evidence to support the diagnosis of chronic fatigue syndrome." In addition, the letter informed me that any restrictions or limitations I had did not prevent me from working since my job was sedentary. The effect of my cognitive symptoms was apparently ignored.

Luckily, I was aware of the law's provision for a "full and fair" internal administrative review of this decision by my insurer (6) and my right to copies of all documents "pertinent" to my denial (6,7). I demanded these immediately. Apparently, all my medical records had been sent for review to a group of doctors who had recommended a denial. The report of these "independent" physicians was both fascinating and abhorrent. Of particular interest, in retrospect, was the doctors' assignment: "Determine if diagnosis is chronic fatigue syndrome or a mental/nervous condition." Like most LTD plans, mine limited benefits to two years for disabilities due to mental illness. Despite no reference to any type of mental illness in any of my medical records, the report concluded that I had "a mental/nervous condition, or a psychosomatic disorder, but definitely not . . . chronic fatigue syndrome." The reviewing doctors totally ignored my abnormal laboratory test results which indicated that *some* disease process had been activated. In addition, they apparently gave no weight to the fact that not only my primary care physician but all consulting physicians who had examined me had no doubt that my symptoms were real and that I truly was disabled. They did, however, make disparaging assumptions about my personal life based solely on old-fashioned male stereotypes of single, professional women. In short, my application for benefits was handled in a manner intended to throw up a roadblock in the hope that I would simply give up on my application.

I did not give up. While the illness made it extremely difficult to assert my rights, I at least knew what needed to be done. Under ERISA, I had sixty days to file an appeal (8). However, I clearly needed an attorney familiar with medical disability issues because I was too sick to handle this on my own. My doctor, who continued to believe I was disabled, was stunned at the denial and, therefore, uncertain as to how to reply to my insurer's report. I discovered that finding a suitable attorney was not easy. However, after many inquiries to friends and colleagues, I finally located one who had successfully taken on insurance claims with CFS as the cause of disability. Until I met with my attorney, I did not know that the CDC had published a working case definition of CFS in the *Annals of Internal Medicine* in 1988 (5).[2] Nor was I aware that this definition, intended for research purposes, was being used by LTD carriers and others to verify a CFS diagnosis. Through him I also learned that CFS was a controversial diagnosis and one that should be avoided. This attorney worked diligently with my doctor, including reviewing all of my medical records. He noted that three tests commonly used to screen for other diseases were repeatedly abnormal. These were not "fancy" tests; they had been around for a long time and results such as mine were considered well-established markers for abnormal immune system activity. In the meantime, my work-up was continuing and I was sent to a cardiologist. He recommended a tilt table test which resulted in a diagnosis of dysautonomia. (This was years before the Johns Hopkins University study on CFS and neurally mediated hypotension was undertaken [9].)

Of particular interest to both my doctor and my attorney was a specific part of the CDC's case definition. According to it,

> Other clinical conditions that may produce similar symptoms must be excluded by thorough evaluation, based on history, physical examination, and appropriate laboratory findings. . . . If any of these tests are abnormal, the physician should search for other conditions that may cause such a result. (5)

Relying on a narrow interpretation of this language, my doctor concluded that I did *not* have CFS. Instead, he opined, dysautonomia and an unspecified immune disorder were responsible for my symptoms. My attorney filed an appeal which explained in detail how my diagnoses were arrived at (as well as how I met the minor criteria and half of the major criteria of the CDC's CFS definition). He also included the results of a psychiatric evaluation which documented that I did not have any kind of mental disorder.

Within three weeks of filing the appeal, my claim was approved.[3] I even received a congratulatory telephone call from my claims analyst, who implied that the objective test results included in this round were key to her company's decision. However, there is nothing in my policy which implies that any test results are necessary to a successful claim. In addition, only the positive tilt test result was new; the abnormal serologic responses were reported in my doctor's initial letter but had been ignored. I believe changing the label from CFS was as key as the test results to this decision. My symptoms had not changed since my initial application, nor had my functional impairments. As to the new diagnosis of dysautonomia, recent research confirms that this is a significant and common component of CFS (10).

To be safe, I underwent the same testing when next reviewed by my insurance company. The results had not changed, nor had any of my symptoms or my ability to function. My doctor recited the same dual diagnoses in his report despite treating me for CFS with gamma globulin shots. His assessment of my continuing disability was accepted without questions by my claims analyst. However, the review following this one was requested while I was seeing a new doctor for more aggressive treatment. This doctor, after careful review of my medical records to date as well as his own physical and laboratory examinations, diagnosed my illness as CFS. He arrived at this conclusion by noting I met the CDC definition's minor criteria as well as the major criteria since no other unifying diagnosis could explain my symptoms. In a lengthy, detailed report, he explained that both dysautonomia and the previously mentioned immune disorder were often seen in CFS patients and, therefore, did not amount to exclusionary diagnoses. For further proof that I had CFS, he pointed to the results of his own, more sophisticated tests of my immune system which showed dysfunction consistent with markers for the illness documented by well-known CFS researchers, including NIH's Dr. Straus (11). He also provided my test-happy insurance reviewers with objective evidence of endocrine and viral disturbances. In addition, he explained how my illness affected my ability to take care of myself, let alone work.

I hoped that a report as packed with laboratory test abnormalities as this one, despite the change to a CFS diagnosis, would pass muster. However, my suspicion that my insurer was biased against CFS claims bore fruit several months later. First, I received an apparently innocuous letter (two years to the date after the start of my benefit eligibility) informing me that my claim was being reviewed to see if I could work at a job outside of my profession (the policy's standard of disability which comes into effect at this time). I was informed that a final determination could not be made until certain unspecified information was received, but that I would continue receiving benefits on a provisional basis until the company made its decision. Two months later, my doctor received a report (attached to a letter from my claims analyst) written by a medical consultant. He was asked to comment on the report and was put on notice that, if he did not do so within 30 days, it would be presumed that he agreed with its findings and conclusions. Notably, the consultant's report clearly was sent to my insurer *four months* earlier (shortly after my doctor recertified my disability status and changed my diagnosis to CFS).

This report concluded that, while I was indeed disabled, my symptoms were due to a parasitic infection, not CFS. Not only did the medical consultant arrive at a different diagnosis based solely on a review of my medical records, he also prescribed a treatment that is so toxic it is only given to dying AIDS patients and others similarly situated. In this doctor's opinion, I could be completely cured and should be able to go back to work within six months. The infection this doctor felt was responsible for my symptoms, however, did not exist. He had attached his diagnoses to titers that indicated a past, not current, infection. They were no more significant as an indicator of causation than elevated Epstein-Barr titers (commonly found in CFS patients) were. The latter had been considered and dismissed as irrelevant by the NIH years ago (5). Apparently, the consultant's report was the strongest basis for a denial my insurer was able to procure. After all, the report had been in the company's possession two months before I was sent the letter stating a decision on my claim could not be made until *more information* was received.

My physician wrote a brief note stating his disagreement with the consultant's report in order to meet the ridiculously short 30-day deadline. A few weeks later, he sent his own detailed report, once again stating I was disabled due to CFS. He noted that the titers on which the consultant (an internist) based his diagnosis had been carefully considered and dismissed as irrelevant by an infectious disease specialist I had seen earlier. A letter from this doctor to my current physician was included which stated there was no evidence of active parasitic infection in any critical organ system which would have to be present for the consultant's diagnosis to be valid. He, as well as my current treating physician, noted that the recommended treatment was extremely toxic and could endanger my life if prescribed under these circumstances. My own doctor pointed out that, ironically, even my insurer's medical consultant was in agreement with his own assessment of the results of the tests he ran on me; namely that my immune system seemed to be fighting an invader of some sort. He also noted that they both concurred that I was severely ill and much too functionally impaired to work at any job.

I would have thought that such a comprehensive response would have satisfied the questions regarding my disability status my insurer posed. Unfortunately, this was not the case. One month later my doctor received yet another letter from my claims analyst. While thanking him for his response, it stated that review of my file determined that, once more, additional information was necessary to ascertain if I continued to qualify for benefits. (By now she had received a one-inch thick stack of objective evidence supporting my illness.) The letter requested copies of his office notes generated since he last submitted them with his original disability certification as well as results of a very specific list of tests. In addition, evidence of my cognitive limitations and their origins was asked for. Once more, he was to respond in 30 days; if he did not meet this deadline, my continuing disability status would be based on what they had on file. Clearly, this was a veiled threat that my benefits could be cut off.

Unfortunately, my doctor had ceased practicing medicine when this letter arrived. I had switched to another physician, but did not receive notice of the letter until after my first office visit with him. (Based on a physical exam, my symptoms, and all of my previous medical records, this doctor confirmed that I had CFS based on the CDC case definition.) Luckily for me, my new doctor knew someone who could do the cognitive status examination. He pointed out that the tests requested by my insurer would, if run on someone like me with a case of CFS, have normal results. Given the history of harassment I had experienced of late with my insurer, he also suggested that my exercise capacity and its effect on me be tested on an exercise bicycle with an attached oxygen monitor. My cortisol level before and after this exercise also would be tested. However, due to his busy practice, these tests could not be scheduled for another six weeks.

My insurance company was informed of this change in circumstances and the scheduling problems by my attorney as well as my new physician. Rather than granting some leeway, the company apparently smelled blood and sent off a letter informing me that my claim had been placed in a "suspend" status and would be terminated if it did not receive the information requested several weeks prior to the date my new doctor was able to supply it. Nothing in ERISA allows for a "suspension" of benefits. I could have considered this a constructive denial of benefits and proceeded with another internal administrative review followed by a lawsuit if the "suspension" was upheld by my insurer. However, proceeding in this manner would have potentially left me without any income for an even longer period of time. I strongly suspect the company was aware of this.

A comprehensive package including results of the bicycle stress test and a cognitive evoked computerized EEG was sent by my new treating physician at the time promised. My insurance company did not send me my monthly benefit check until it received this information. (Luckily, the check was delayed only one week.) These tests, as well as additional ones undertaken to assess treatment options, provided strong objective evidence of severe disability (as had been claimed by all doctors consulted). My doctor also wrote a lengthy letter explaining his evaluation, testing, treatment and follow-up of me to date.

I did not hear from my claims analyst for several months. During this time, my benefits were paid in the usual manner. The next event affecting

my LTD benefits was my long-awaited SSDI award.[4] This favorable decision by the SSA resulted in a flurry of correspondence while my LTD
award was adjusted to reflect my monthly SSDI benefits, as called for in
the policy. Since then, I have received periodic requests from my insurer
for updates on my disability status. While some of my symptoms have
changed (some increasing in severity, others decreasing), my overall ability to function has not. In fact, in some areas I have declined. My doctor
completes his sections of the insurance forms and I fill out mine. These, as
well as the objective data regarding my physical and neurocognitive deficits and my SSDI award seem to have satisfied my LTD insurance carrier–
so far.

My experience indicates that CFS is not a respected diagnosis among
LTD carriers. I find it interesting that a co-worker, diagnosed with lupus
(and currently receiving benefits through the same group insurance policy
as I), has not been subjected to the kind of delays and questioning as I was
at any time. She, too, has objective evidence of abnormal immune system
activity. Notably, her symptoms are remarkably similar to mine as is her
functional impairment in general (although her symptoms actually go into
remission for relatively long periods of time). Despite sending evidence to
our insurer which sometimes shows improved functional capacity, she has
never experienced an interruption of benefits or any threats of such action.

Unfortunately, constant reevaluation of my condition has not resulted in
a well-known and respected diagnosis like hers. Clearly, an established
diagnosis makes a difference. The manner in which my insurer handled
my claim provides ample evidence that it was fishing for a diagnosis other
than CFS. For example, the specific tests it outlined in its last request
would not have helped assess my functional capacity; they are used purely
for diagnostic purposes. Evidently, my insurer, like many, was uncomfort-
able about establishing a precedent by paying benefits for a CFS claim.
Other insurers seem to feel the same way. Recently, several have received
permission from state insurance commissions to limit LTD benefits to two
years for illnesses lacking objective markers (in their new or renewed
contracts with employers) (12). The importance of continued federally-
funded research to establish such markers for CFS cannot be understated.
In addition, since insurers seem baffled by the many variations of CFS,
government-supported studies stratified according to research subjects'
illness severity as well as symptomology (e.g., primarily immunologic,
neurologic, etc.) would be extremely helpful to all concerned.

While diseases like lupus and multiple sclerosis are more easily diagnosed than CFS because of their well-recognized markers, they, too, can
vary in symptomology and severity. Disability insurers must have ways to

assess functional impairment in claimants with these more established illnesses. Applying such well-recognized means of measuring disability to CFS would assist patients, their doctors, and LTD carriers. (My insurer never indicated what type of testing would help in evaluating my claim.) In addition, LTD insurers should recognize and respect the in-depth knowledge treating physicians have about their patients. These doctors' evaluations of their patients' ability to work are based on established and on-going physician-patient relationships and should be weighed accordingly. If an occasion arises where a third-party medical assessment appears necessary, the treating doctor and LTD insurer should work together and choose a truly *independent* consultant familiar with and up-to-date on the current scientific status of CFS.

Changes in the law are also necessary to ensure that those who are covered by employer-provided LTD policies are entitled to the same rights and remedies as individual LTD policyholders.[5] In the meantime, it is important for CFS claimants to make sure that the information submitted to their insurer contains as strong evidence as possible to prove disability.[6] This is the record on which the insurer makes its decision, and, in most cases, it is difficult, if not impossible, to add new evidence to it once a case is in court. Because of the importance of this administrative record, it is imperative that physicians treating LTD claimants with CFS understand that their office notes (while intended only as a record to refresh their own recollection of their patients' status) will be scrutinized by LTD carriers looking for a chance to deny benefits. For example, had the doctor who first detected the possibility of a parasitic infection in my case written down his reasons for dismissing this diagnosis, my insurer may not have challenged my claim with its consultant's report.

Despite problems with ERISA, the law does provide important protections if benefits are refused on an unreasonable basis. For example, pursuing an administrative appeal allows more evidence to be brought in which the insurer is legally obligated to consider. In addition, an improper denial at this stage is unlikely to be upheld in court. If the administrator of the LTD plan does not have discretionary authority to interpret the plan (and many don't), the court will review the decision to deny benefits *de novo—* basically ignoring the plan administrator's denial and deciding on its own whether the claim should be paid based on the insurance policy's rules and the evidence presented (13). In cases where the administrator is granted discretion regarding plan interpretation, the court will ascertain if this discretion has been abused (taking into account the administrator's potential conflict of interest) (13). ERISA also allows claimants who are successful in litigation to petition the court to recover their attorney's fees and costs from the defendant (14).[7] Bad faith is generally considered in deciding whether to grant such a request, as well as the deterrent effect of such an award on others.[8] Therefore, such an award has not only the effect of punishing the insurer but also warns others to comply with the law.

In conclusion, the current manner of determining eligibility for disability benefits for someone with a diagnosis of chronic fatigue syndrome is unnecessarily difficult for all. For the physician, it entails more paperwork than he or she bargained for, difficulties in conveying the functional impact of the patient's illness, and, more often than not, deliberate misinterpretation of medical records. If the patient retains an attorney, this advocate is caught in the frustrating situation of realizing the insurer often is acting in bad faith, yet can actually get away with this behavior legally. However, the biggest burden of the process falls upon the patient, who is ill, functioning at a low level, and often without his or her former cognitive skills. For the patient, the process is humiliating, exhausting, and at times, results in a lengthier and more severe period of disablement. Thus, ironically, LTD insurers may end up increasing their financial obligations as a result of the manner in which they handle CFS claims.

NOTES

1. See *Firestone Tire & Rubber Co. v. Bruch,* 489 U.S. 101, 115 (1989). If the plan administrator has discretionary authority to interpret the plan, the court will look for an abuse of this discretion. In general, abuse of discretion has been interpreted as arbitrary and capricious behavior. See, e.g., *Sansevera v. E. I. DuPont de Nemours & Co.,* 859 F. Supp. 106, 110-11 (S.D.N.Y. 1994).

2. This CDC case definition was revised in 1994. See Fukuda K, Straus SE, Hickie I, et al. The chronic fatigue syndrome: A comprehensive approach to its definition and study. *Ann Int Med* 1994;121:953-959.

3. It took another 30 months for my SSDI application to be approved. Thus, had I not been covered by a private disability insurance plan, I would not have had any income for three years.

4. The SSA also requested a mental status assessment while reviewing my SSDI application. This evaluation was composed of neurocognitive testing (which showed clear deficits) as well as an MMPI (which again documented the absence of any mental illness). Had the agency succeeded in its effort to define my illness as mental and awarded benefits on such a diagnosis, my LTD carrier surely would have taken note and limited its financial obligation to me to two years.

5. The latter may sue under state contract or tort law for compensatory and/or punitive damages if their claims are improperly processed.

6. Applicants for LTD benefits should be careful to keep copies of all correspondence with their insurer and communicate only in writing as verbal communications may be misconstrued and end up as notes in the insurance claim file. In

addition, applicants may want to limit the insurer's authorization for release of information before signing to assure only pertinent records are gathered.

7. Attorney's fees and costs generated while applying for benefits and pursuing an administrative appeal may be included in a fee award. *Pennsylvania v. Delaware Valley Citizens' Council for Clean Air,* 478 U.S. 546, 560 (1986).

8. *See, e.g., Hummell v. Rykoff & Co.,* 634 F.2d 446, 453 (9th Cir. 1980).

REFERENCES

1. 29 U.S.C. §1001-1461 (1996).

2. *Pilot Life Ins. Co. v. Dedeaux,* 481 U.S. 41, 52 (1987).

3. *Metropolitan Life Ins. Co. v. Taylor,* 481 U.S. 58, 62 (1987).

4. 29 C.F.R. §2560.503-1(e)(3).

5. Holmes GP, Kaplan JE, Gantz NM, et al. Chronic fatigue syndrome: a working case definition. *Ann Intern Med* 1988;108:387-389.

6. 29 U.S.C. §1133(2).

7. 29 C.F.R. §2560.503-1(g)(1).

8. 29 C.F.R. §2560.503-1(g)(3).

9. Bou-Houlaigah I, Rowe P, Kan J, Calkins H. The relationship between neurally-mediated hypotension and the chronic fatigue syndrome. *JAMA* 1995;274: 961-967.

10. Freeman R, Komaroff AL. Does the chronic fatigue syndrome involve the autonomic nervous system? *Am J Med* 1997;102:357-364.

11. Straus SE, Fritz S, Dale JK, Gould B, Strober W. Lymphocyte phenotype and function in the chronic fatigue syndrome. *J Clin Immunol* 1993;13:30-40.

12. Jeffrey, NA. Insurers Curb Some Benefits For Disability. *Wall Street Journal* July 25, 1996:A3.

13. *Firestone Tire & Rubber Co. v. Bruch,* 489 U.S. 101, 115 (1989).

14. 29 U.S.C. §1132(g)(1).

Index

Note: Page numbers followed by the letter "t" designate tables; and numbers followed by the letter "f" designate figures.

Haworth
DOCUMENT DELIVERY
SERVICE

This valuable service provides a single-article order form for any article from a Haworth journal.

- *Time Saving:* No running around from library to library to find a specific article.
- *Cost Effective:* All costs are kept down to a minimum.
- *Fast Delivery:* Choose from several options, including same-day FAX.
- *No Copyright Hassles:* You will be supplied by the original publisher.
- *Easy Payment:* Choose from several easy payment methods.

Open Accounts Welcome for ...
- Library Interlibrary Loan Departments
- Library Network/Consortia Wishing to Provide Single-Article Services
- Indexing/Abstracting Services with Single Article Provision Services
- Document Provision Brokers and Freelance Information Service Providers

---

MAIL or *FAX* THIS ENTIRE ORDER FORM TO:

Haworth Document Delivery Service
The Haworth Press, Inc.
10 Alice Street
Binghamton, NY 13904-1580

or FAX: 1-800-895-0582
or CALL: 1-800-342-9678
9am-5pm EST

PLEASE SEND ME PHOTOCOPIES OF THE FOLLOWING SINGLE ARTICLES:

1) Journal Title: _____

    Vol/Issue/Year: _____ Starting & Ending Pages: _____

Article Title: _____

2) Journal Title: _____

    Vol/Issue/Year: _____ Starting & Ending Pages: _____

Article Title: _____

3) Journal Title: _____

    Vol/Issue/Year: _____ Starting & Ending Pages: _____

Article Title: _____

4) Journal Title: _____

    Vol/Issue/Year: _____ Starting & Ending Pages: _____

Article Title: _____

(See other side for Costs and Payment Information)

COSTS: Please figure your cost to order quality copies of an article.

1. Set-up charge per article: $8.00
   ($8.00 × number of separate articles) _____

2. Photocopying charge for each article:

   1-10 pages: $1.00 _____

   11-19 pages: $3.00 _____

   20-29 pages: $5.00 _____

   30+ pages: $2.00/10 pages _____

3. Flexicover (optional): $2.00/article _____

4. Postage & Handling: US: $1.00 for the first article/
   $.50 each additional article _____

   Federal Express: $25.00 _____

   Outside US: $2.00 for first article/
   $.50 each additional article_____

5. Same-day FAX service: $.35 per page _____

   GRAND TOTAL: _____

METHOD OF PAYMENT: (please check one)

❑ Check enclosed   ❑ Please ship and bill. PO # _____
(sorry we can ship and bill to bookstores only! All others must pre-pay)

❑ Charge to my credit card: ❑ Visa; ❑ MasterCard; ❑ Discover;
   ❑ American Express;

Account Number:_____ Expiration date:_____

Signature: ✗_____

Name: _____ Institution: _____

Address: _____

_____

City: _____ State:_____ Zip:_____

Phone Number: _____ FAX Number: _____

MAIL or *FAX* THIS ENTIRE ORDER FORM TO:

Haworth Document Delivery Service	**or FAX:** 1-800-895-0582
The Haworth Press, Inc.	**or CALL:** 1-800-342-9678
10 Alice Street	9am-5pm EST)
Binghamton, NY 13904-1580	